Jessie Rice Sandberg

SWORD OF THE LORD PUBLISHERS
Box 1099, Murfreesboro, Tennessee 37130

ISBN 0-87398-927-9

Printed and bound in the United States of America

TO MY OWN CAROL

WITH LOVE AND A PINCH OF SALT

A scrapbook of recipes, poems, ideas, and essays for the new bride, the bored housewife, the frantic mother, the curious husband and the woman who wants to be better than she is.

Beautiful for Thee

J. Sandberg

Lord, make me beau-ti-ful for Thee— Beau-ti-ful for Thee. A meek and qui-et spir-it, A pure and lov-ing heart. Hands that do Thy will and lips that tell how great Thou art. Lord, make me beau-ti-ful for Thee— Oh, beau-ti-ful for Thee.

Presented to

----

by

Date

TABLE OF CONTENTS

Desserts

WHAT A WOMAN!

I see a mother stand by a bed
And pray, no matter what the doctor has said,
And faithfully lays cool cloths to the head
Of the little patient she won't let be dead;
And I say, "What a woman!"

I see a teacher patiently go
Once more through the words so the child will know,
And urges and listens 'til the new words flow
From the pupil from whom she won't take No;
And I say, "What a woman!"

I see a judge rise to the crest of jurisprudence above the rest,
With all her genius put to the test
And she stays calm and undistressed;
And I say, "What a woman!"

I see a mountain girl disdain
Her one-room poverty and pain,
To teach her husband each refrain
Of Bible verses for his gain,
And rear four sons from out the mire
As preachers, others to inspire,
And so instill in them a fire
Of holy zeal that will not tire;
And I say, "What a woman!"

A woman! to be one is not
A shameful or degrading lot
At judge's bench or cooking pot,
If her course by God's will is plot.
She can by virtue elevate
The charismata of her state
'Til watchers will admire her fate
And say when she walks through the gate
Of Heaven, "What a woman!"

—Bill Harvey
October, 1975.

. . .ON SETTING GOALS

Among all the living things of earth, human beings alone have the ability to consciously shape the time that lies between the biological markers of birth and death. We alone have the ability to decide not only what we will make of our lives, but to change our minds about what we will make of them. This ability is affected, of course, by the circumstances in which we find ourselves. We can't ignore the effect of the outer world on our inner selves—but neither can we afford to let the external world impose on us a lifestyle or life goals that violate our internal needs.

—Nena O'Neill.

ASPIRATIONS

"I do not like the phrase: Never cross a bridge till you come to it. The world is owned by men who cross bridges on their imaginations miles and miles in advance of the procession."

—Bruce Barton.

"There is never much trouble in any family where the children hope someday to resemble their parents."

—William Lyon Phelps.

"I like to see a man proud of the place in which he lives. I like to see a man live so that his place will be proud of him."

—Abraham Lincoln.

50 WAYS TO STAY HAPPY

1. Tell someone how much you appreciate him/her.
2. Memorize the first seven verses of Psalm 37.
3. Invite a neighbor over for a cup of coffee.
4. Listen to a favorite recording.
5. Write a letter to someone who is lonely.
6. Make a list of all the things you are thankful for.
7. Offer to babysit for a young mother with several small children.
8. Make a batch of fudge for someone who wouldn't expect it.
9. Ask your pastor for a job to do.
10. Subscribe to a good Christian paper or magazine.
11. Learn something new—sewing, furniture refinishing, ceramics.
12. Make a collection of your best recipes for a new bride.
13. Make a fancy coffeecake for a new neighbor.

14. Invite someone new over after church on Sunday.
15. Take fifteen minutes everyday for some kind of exercise besides housework.
16. Come to breakfast looking as pretty as you can!
17. Tell your husband how glad you are that he picked you out.
18. Compliment your children about something, sincerely!
19. Do a special private study on some book of the Bible.
20. Wake your husband tomorrow with a kiss.
21. Try writing a poem.
22. Make a doll dress for a favorite little girl.
23. Plan a "finger supper" for your family to enjoy in front of the TV.
24. Plant a windowsill garden.
25. Design a funny get-well card for someone in the hospital.
26. Spend half a day in an old people's home just listening to them talk.
27. Make a prayer list. Record every answer to prayer.
28. Try a new recipe for dinner tonight.
29. Send a note to your child's teacher telling her how much you appreciate her work.
30. Smile at everyone you meet today.
31. Re-arrange a room.
32. Light candles and use your best china for an ordinary family dinner.
33. Let your children invite their friends over in the afternoon for a taffy pull.
34. Cultivate a new friend.
35. Buy a craft magazine for patterns. Start making birthday presents instead of buying them.
36. Get a library card. Use it!
37. Try reading the Bible through in a year.
38. Be especially nice to the check-out clerk in the grocery store.
39. Stop and look at your children. Notice how beautiful and sweet they are.
40. Try a new hair style.
41. Put a note in your husband's pocket telling him how great you think he is!
42. Tackle some job you've dreaded doing and finish it up as quickly as you can.
43. Have a tea party with your toddler; try hard to forget the housework for a little while.
44. Set some goals for yourself and check off everyone you accomplish.
45. Help your children make a puppet theatre out of a cardboard box. Make finger puppets.
46. Take a hot bath (with bath oil); close your eyes and relax.

47. Put on a little cologne before dinner tonight. Even the children enjoy a mommy who smells nice.
48. Memorize the words to a hymn which has meant a great deal to you.
49. Put a surprise in the children's lunch boxes.
50. Tell someone how good the Lord has been to you.

A SET OF LIFETIME GOALS FOR THE CHRISTIAN WIFE AND MOTHER

1. To be a regular, effective witness for the Lord; SOUL WINNING.
2. To develop an always-increasing hunger for the Lord Jesus.
3. To be a consistent influence for good among those whose lives I touch day by day.
4. To help my husband, by my love and prayers and my careful attention to home responsibilities, to be the best possible man of God he can be.
5. To do everything in my power to help my children be of outstanding character, well-educated both mentally and spiritually, concerned about the needs of other people, and totally committed to a life of service for the Lord Jesus Christ.
6. To have a deep and genuine love for other people and to know how to express that love in practical and meaningful ways.
7. To learn to accept myself as God made me; to improve those areas I am able to improve and then to leave my limitations and failures with the Lord.
8. To enjoy and use the gift of time to the fullest possible measure. To learn to find joy in immediate pleasures and daily responsibilities. To avoid wasting time in anger or bitterness or self-pity; to practice an hourly "rejoicing in the Lord" regardless of circumstances.
9. To learn how to pray and to spend time in prayer to the extent that I will regularly see results in my own life and in the lives of others for whom I am concerned.
10. To be a growing, interesting, always learning, always enthusiastic person; to work at developing new opportunities and new ideas, keeping abreast of what is happening in the world and seeking solutions and answers to the world's needs.
11. To have a thorough and practical knowledge of the Word of God, to make it the moment-by-moment guide in my own life and to teach it to others; to memorize large portions of it and to know references for ready access to its riches; to find a daily joy in its study.
12. To seriously consider my gifts and to find ways of developing and using them in service for the Lord as well as a means toward personal

fulfillment and a more intense satisfaction with my life.

13. To keep a strong sensitivity to sin; to constantly seek for purity of heart; to make a daily practice of heart-searching and confession of sin.

14. To come to the last day of my life with a sense of "completeness" in the Lord Jesus; that there be no sense of futility or wasted purposes to mar my joy and expectation in seeing my Saviour, face to face.

—Jessie Sandberg.

DO I HAVE PROBLEMS WITH OTHER PEOPLE BECAUSE:

1. I am too sensitive and overreact?
2. I tend to say whatever I feel regardless of the consequences?
3. I tend to remember the slights and mistreatments of others?
4. My voice is too loud?
5. I answer back to people too quickly?
6. I excuse myself when I take out my frustrations and discomforts on other people?
7. I am stingy with my smiles?
8. I tend toward a sour disposition?
9. I try to "get even" when I have been mistreated?
10. I remind others of their failures?
11. I frequently feel misunderstood?
12. I always see the difficulties in every situation?
13. It is hard for me to be kind to those who are beneath my station?
14. I tend to complain and nag?
15. I dislike giving credit where credit is due?

HERE IS THE SOLUTION TO MY PROBLEM:

"Let all bitterness, and wrath, and anger, and clamour, and evil speaking, be put away from you, with all malice: And be ye kind one to another, tenderhearted, forgiving one another, even as God for Christ's sake hath forgiven you."—Eph. 4:31,32.

PRACTICAL HELPS TOWARD GOOD SELF-ESTEEM

1. Replace uncomfortable feelings with some comfortable ones. Think positively.
2. Learn techniques of good conversation. Practice on others.
3. Examine yourself. Face facts of strengths and weaknesses. Develop your strengths.

4. Develop skills. Become as competent as you can in at least one skill.
5. Get experience (doing a thing over and over to help you get rid of shyness and uneasiness.
6. Practice being cordial. Learn good manners and appropriate dress.
7. Learn to laugh at your own mistakes. Who said you can't make one?
8. Read two or three books each year on personality development.
9. Develop an interest in many people. You can do this if you try to see others through God's eyes.
10. Reach out to two or three new persons daily (smile, speak, encourage, show genuine interest).

—Mrs. Douglas Cravens.

QUICK ENERGY PICKUPS

1. Borrow a child's jump rope and skip rope in the fresh air as often as you find the time.
2. Walk—or better still, run—around the block, taking deep breaths of air.
3. Train yourself to take instant naps of no longer than 20 minutes. Next best, lie down and relax completely for the same length of time.
4. Take a cold shower. If you're tired and tense, take a warm bath first, followed by the cold shower.
5. Steal a snack from your breakfast to have mid-morning. Do the same thing at lunch and dinner.
6. Plan and eat one day's menus without repeating a single food you've had all month.
7. Eat sunflower seeds for between-meal snacks.
8. Change your routine. Do something entirely different. Take a course in painting. Volunteer your services to a school, a hospital. Walk down a new road.
9. Contribute an hour to a cause you care about and could become deeply involved in. Don't wait until you have more time. Do it now!
10. Assign one of your duties to another family member. In the saved time, do something just because you enjoy it.

—By Lee Parr McGrath,
"How to Recharge Your Energy,"
Family Circle Magazine, November '72

10 WAYS TO CUT DOWN ON STRESS

(*Type A Behavior and Your Heart*, Meyer Friedman, M. D., and Ray Rosenman, M.D.)

1. Plan some idleness every day.
2. Listen to others without interruption.
3. Read books that demand concentration.
4. Learn to savor food.
5. Have a place for retreat at home.
6. Avoid irritating, overly competitive people.
7. Plan leisurely, less-structured vacations.
8. Concentrate on enriching yourself.
9. Live by the calendar, not the stopwatch.
10. Concentrate on one task at a time.

A MENTAL HEALTH CHECK-UP (Menninger Foundation)

1. What are my goals in life; how realistic are they?
2. Is my use of time and energy helping me to reach these goals?
3. Do I have a proper sense of responsibility or do I try to do too much and fail to acknowledge my limitations?
4. How do I react to disappointments and losses?
5. How am I coping with stress and anxiety?
6. What is the consistency and quality of my personal relationships?
7. From whom do I receive and to whom do I give emotional support? Do I avoid getting support from others for fear of appearing weak?
8. What is the role of love in my life? How much time do I give to listen to and care for others?

—From *U. S. News and World Report* May, 1976.

HOW TO LIVE LIFE AT YOUR BEST POTENTIAL

1. See yourself as God sees you.
2. Start where you are. Make yourself available to Him.
3. Eliminate any sin in your life.
4. Align your will with God's.
5. Plan exciting activities.
6. Set goals for your life—realistic, short and long-range, interesting goals. Ask: Where am I heading?

7. Ask the Lord to keep your attitude right.

All of us face comparable times of pressure and crisis. We must immediately evaluate relative priorities, then give our undivided attention first to the one which requires the more immediate attention. At the same time we must refuse to feel the pressure of the other situation until we are able to give our attention to it.

—From *Run and Not Be Weary*,
Dwight L. Carlson, M. D., p. 198.

If you live in the street called Now, in a house named Here—
If you live at number Here North Now Street, let us say,
Then immediate things, discomfort, sorrow, it is clear,
Are of first importance; you could feel no other way.
But if you pitch your tent each evening nearer the town
Of your true desire, and glimpse its gates less far,
Then you lay you down on nettles, you lay you down
With vipers, and you scarcely notice where you are.
The world is not relinquished; but the world assumes
Its proper place in that perspective, is not all;
Is harsh with envy, greed, assault,— or blooms
With friendship, courage, truth, is beautiful;
Yet is at best but an inn on a thoroughfare:
Provincial, one might call the mind contented there.
            —Edna St. Vincents Millay
            from "Conversation at Midnight."

A LESSON
I walked a mile with Pleasure.
She chatted all the way;
But left me none the wiser
    For all she had to say.

I walked a mile with Sorrow;
And not a word said she,
But Oh! the things I learned from her,
    When Sorrow walked with me.
        —Author unknown.

BIBLIOGRAPHY OF BOOKS FOR WOMEN

We do not give an unqualified recommendation of all these books. However, they are books that can meet many needs of women. Will you read them prayerfully and use that which will be a blessing to you and your family?

I. CHRISTIAN HOME AND FAMILY

Adams, Jay. *Christian Living in the Home.*
Adams, Jay. *Godliness Through Discipline.*
Baker. *The Happy Housewife.*
Bouma. *The Creative Homemaker.*
Brandt, Henry. *Build a Happy Home with Discipline.*
Brandt, Henry. *Building a Christian Home.*
Brandt, Henry. *Six Talks on Family Living.*
Christenson, Larry. *The Christian Family.*
Clarkson, E. Margaret. *Susie's Babies.*
Cooper. *You Can Be the Wife of a Happy Husband.*
Davis, Clifford. *Your Family and God.*
Dobson, James. *Discipline with Love.*
Dobson, James. *Dare to Discipline.*
Dobson, James. *Hide and Seek* (How to Build Self-Esteem in Your Child).
Gangel, Kenneth. *The Family First.*
Hancock, Maxine. *Love, Honor, and Be Free.*
Handford, Elizabeth. *Me? Obey Him?*
Hardesty, Margaret. *Forever My Love.* (a must for your husband).
Hendricks, Howard. *Heaven Help the Home.*
Hunt, Gladys. *Honey for a Child's Heart.*
Hyles, Jack. *How to Rear Children.*
Hyles, Jack. *Satan's Bid for Your Child.*
LaHaye, Tim. *How to Be Happy Though Married.*
Landorf, Joyce. *His Stubborn Love.*
Lunford, Bob. *How to Be Happily Married.*
Mallory. *The Kink and I.*
Miller, Ella. *Happiness is Homemaking.*
Narramore, Bruce. *Help! I'm a Parent.*
Narramore, Clyde. *Counseling Youth.*
Narramore, Clyde. *Discipline in the Christian Home.*
Narramore, Clyde. *How to Begin and Improve Family Devotions.*
Narramore, Clyde. *How to Help Your Child Develop Faith in God.*
Narramore, Clyde. *How to Succeed in Family Living.*
Narramore, Clyde. *How to Tell Your Children About Sex.*
Narramore, Clyde. *How to Understand and Influence Children.*

Narramore, Clyde. *Is Your Child Gifted?*
Narramore, Clyde. *Understanding and Guiding Teenagers.*
Narramore, Clyde. *Young Children and Their Problems.*
Narramore, Clyde. *Understanding Your Children.*
Orr. *How to Get Along With Your Teens.*
Orr. *How to Keep Your Husband Happy.*
Orr. *Seven Rules For a Happy Christian Home.*
Orr. *What to Teach Young Children.*
Osbourn, Cecil. *The Art of Understanding Your Mate.*
Peterson, Allan. *The Marriage Affair.*
Pyle, Hugh. *The Taming of the Teenager.*
Pyle, Hugh. *The Taming of the Toddler.*
Renich, Jill. *To Have and to Hold.*
Rice, Cathy. *The Right Romance in Marriage.*
Rice, John R. *God in Your Home.*
Rice, John R. *The Home: Courtship, Marriage, and Children.*
Rice, Shirley. *Physical Unity in Marriage.*
Rice, Shirley. *The Christian Home.*
Scorer, C. G. *The Bible and Sex Ethics Today.*
Shaw and Johnson. *Your Children.*
Shedd, Charlie. *Talk to Me.*
Strauss, Richard. *Marriage Is for Love.*
Swift, Henry and Elizabeth. *Running a Happy Family.*
Trent, Robbie. *Your Child and God.*
Trobisch, Walter. *I Married You.*
Vandenburch. *Fill Your Days With Life.* (over 60 years)
Whiston, Lionel. *Marriage Is for Living.*
Wagermaker, Herbert. *Why Can't I Understand My Kids?*
Wonderley, Gustava. *Training Children.*
Wyrtzen, Jack. *Sex and the Bible.*
Wyrtzen, Jack. *Sex Is Not Sinful.*

II. CHRISTIAN CHARACTER

Adams, Jay. *Christ and Your Problems.*
Adams, Jay. *What to Do About Worry.*
Adolph, Paul. *Health Shall Spring Forth.*
Atwood, Grace. *Beauty Is Soul Deep.*
Barrett, Ethel. *Don't Look Now but Your Personality Is Showing.*
Baughman, Ray. *The Abundant Life.*
Blaiklock. *Release From Tension.*
Collins, Gary. *A Psychologist Looks at Life.* (Anxiety, Loneliness, Guilt, Frustration, Inferiority, Discouragement, Anger, Emptiness).

Douglas, Mack R. *How to Make a Habit of Succeeding.*
Engstrom and MacKenzie. *Managing Your Time.*
Haggai, John Edmund. *How to Win Over Worry.*
Hunt, Gladys. *Ms. Means Myself.* (Self-esteem).
Koopman, Leroy. *Beauty for the Tongue.*
LaHaye, Tim. *How to Win Over Depression.*
LaHaye, Tim. *Spirit Controlled Temperament.*
LaHaye, Tim. *Transformed Temperament.*
Landorf, Joyce. *The Fragrance of Beauty.*
Landorf, Joyce. *The Richest Woman in Town.*
Lewis, Clifford. *God's Ideal Woman.*
Miller, Ella May. *I Am a Woman.*
Narramore, Clyde. *A Woman's World.*
Narramore, Clyde. *Improving Your Self-Confidence.*
Narramore, Clyde. *Life and Love.* (A Christian View of Sex)
Narramore, Clyde. *Love Is a Feeling to Be Learned.*
Narramore, Clyde. *This Way to Happiness.*
Nee, Watchman. *The Normal Christian Life.*
Parrott, Leslie. *Easy to Live With.*
Pentecost, Dorothy. *My Pursuit of Peace.*
Peterson, Mr. and Mrs. Allan, ed. *For Women Only.*
Ryrie, Charles. *Balancing the Christian Life.*
Sanders, J. Oswald. *Cultivation of Christian Character.*
Sanders, J. Oswald. *A Spiritual Clinic.*
Sanders, J. Oswald. *Spiritual Leadership.*
Schaeffer, Edith. *Hidden Art.*
Smith, Hannah Whitall. *The Christian's Secret of a Happy Life.*
Stanford, Miles J. *Principles of Spiritual Growth.*
Weiss, G. Christian. *On Being a Real Christian.*
Whiston, Lionel. *Are You Fun to Live With?*

III. THE WIFE AND CHRISTIAN SERVICE

Blackwood, Mrs. Andrew. *The Minister's Wife.*
Hewitt, Arthur. *The Shepherdess.*
Nyberg, Kathleen. *The Care and Feeding of Ministers.*
Parrott, Lora Lee. *How to Be a Preacher's Wife and Like It.*
Pentecost, Dorothy. *The Pastor's Wife and the Church.*
Tuggy, Joy. *The Missionary Wife and Her Work.*

IV. DEVOTIONAL BOOKS

Anderson, Evelyn. *Devotionals for Today's Women.*
Carmichael, Amy. *His Thoughts Said. . .His Father Said. . .*
Carmichael, Amy. *If.*

Chambers, Oswald. *My Utmost for His Highest.*
Green, Marge. *Martha, Martha.*
Griffiths, Michael. *Take My Life.*
Holsinger, Elsie. *Thoughts for Young Mothers.*
Kane, H. Victor. *Devotions for Dieters.*
Lockerbie, Jeanette. *Salt in My Kitchen.*
Marshall, Catherine. *Friends With God.*
Price, Eugenia. *The Wider Place.*
Sandberg, Jessie. *Fill My Cup, Lord!*
Sandberg, Jessie. *From My Kitchen Window.*
Spurgeon, Charles. *Morning and Evening.*
Thomas, Ian. *The Mystery of Godliness.*

V. MISCELLANEOUS

Albrecht, Margaret. *A Complete Guide for the Working Mother.*
Bureau of Narcotics and Dangerous Drugs, U. S. Department of Justice, Washington, D.C. 20537. *Drugs of Abuse.*
Laird, Donald and Eleanor. *The Technique of Getting Things Done.*
Laird, Donald and Eleanor. *The Technique of Handling People.*
McMillen, S. L. *None of These Diseases.*
Vanderbilt, Amy. *New Complete Book of Etiquette.*
Wald, Oletta. *The Joy of Discovery in Bible Study, in Bible Teaching.*

VI. CHRISTIAN FICTION

Alcock, Deborah. *The Spanish Brothers.*
Arnold, Francena. *Not My Will.*
Barrett, Ethel. *Holy War.*
Briggs, Argye M. *Root Out of a Dry Ground.*
Connor, Ralph. *Black Rock.*
Connor, Ralph. *The Sky Pilot.*
Dubuar, Helen. *The Master's Touch.*
Epp, Margaret. *A Fountain Sealed.*
Hunter, James M. *Mystery of Mar Saba.*
Hunter, James. *Thine Is the Kingdom.*
Ingles, James Wesley. *Fair Are the Meadows.*
Ingles, James. *Silver Trumpet.*
Johnson, James. *Code Name Sebastian.*
Jones, Bob, Jr. *Wine of Morning.*
Landorf, Joyce. *His Stubborn Love.*
Maier, Paul. *Pontius Pilate.*
Marshall, Catherine. *Christy.*
Matson, Ethel. *Ruth Trent.*

Minshal, Vera. *The Doctor's Secret.*
Moore, Bertha. *Mercy Forever.*
Pryor, Adel. *Her Secret Fear.*
Rice, John R. *Seeking a City.*
Sheldon, Charles. *In His Steps.*
Watson, Sidney. *In the Twinkling of an Eye.*
Watson, Sidney. *The Mark of the Beast.*
Wiggin, Kate. *The Bird's Christmas Carol.*
Wilson, Augusta J. *St. Elmo.*
Woodrum, Lon. *Of Men and of Angels.*
Woodrum, Lon. *Trumpets in the Morning.*
Wright, Harold. *The Re-Creation of Brian Kent.*
Wright, Harold. *The Shepherd of the Hills.*
Wright, Harold. *When a Man's a Man.*
Wyckoff, Albert C. *Bright Horizons.*

VII. CHRISTIAN BIOGRAPHY

Aylward, Gladys. *The Small Woman.*
Bonar, A. A. *The Biography of Robert Murray McCheyne.*
Elliot, Elizabeth. *Shadow of the Almighty.* (Jim Elliot)
Elliot, Elizabeth. *Through Gates of Splendor.*
Goforth, Rosalind. *Climbing.*
Goforth, Rosalind. *Goforth of China.*
Grubbs, Norman. *Once Caught, No Escape.*
Houghton, Frank. *Amy Carmichael of Dohnavur.*
Kuhn, Isobel. *By Searching.*
Kuhn, Isobel. *In the Arena.*
Mathews, Basil. *Livingstone, the Pathfinder.*
Marshall, Catherine. *A Man Called Peter.*
Martin, Roger. *R. A. Torrey, Apostle of Certainty.*
Miller, Basil. *Mary Slessor, Heroine of Calabar.*
Moody, William. *The Life of D. L. Moody.*
Pierson, Arthur. *George Muller of Bristol.*
Powell, Emma M. *Heavenly Destiny.* (life of Mrs. D. L. Moody).
Smith, Hannah. *For Heaven's Sake.*
Sumner, Robert. *Man Sent From God.*
Stull, Ruth. *Sand and Stars.*
Taylor, Howard. *Hudson Taylor's Spiritual Secret.*
Taylor, Mrs. Howard. *The Triumph of John and Betty Stam.*
ten Boom, Corrie. *The Hiding Place.*
ten Boom, Corrie. *Tramp for the Lord.*
Wesley, J. *Journal of John Wesley.*

VIII. THE SINGLE WOMAN

Andrews, Gini. *Your Half of the Apple.*

Fryling, Alice. "The Grace of Single Living," *His Magazine,* February, 1973.

Griffiths, Michael. *Take My Life.*

Hunt, Gladys. *Ms. Means Myself.*

Jepson, Sarah. *For the Love of Singles.*

Narramore, Clyde. *The Unmarried Woman.*

Sands, Audrey Lee. *Single and Satisfied.*

IX. THE ENGAGED

Florio, Anthony. *Two to Get Ready.*

Miles, Herbert J. *Sexual Understanding Before Marriage.*

Miles, Herbert J. *The Dating Game.*

Murray, Alfred L. *Youth's Marriage Problems.*

Narramore, Clyde. *Life and Love.*

Peterson, Allan and Smith, Joyce. *Before You Marry* (Bible Studies for Singles).

Getting Ready

THE CHRISTIAN ENGAGEMENT

INTRODUCTION:

Good communication before marriage is a must! If lack of good communication is the primary cause of divorce, an engaged couple must develop a good and growing communication before marriage. The best ways to develop this are to listen to the other and to talk (really share oneself) with the other. There are hundreds of things to share; therefore, it does take time.

I. WHAT SHOULD YOU TALK ABOUT? Here are a few important topics. They are not listed in order of importance.

1. The health of each.
2. Finances (before and after marriage).
3. Children and homelife.
4. In-laws.
5. Relationships between each of you with your parents and prospective in-laws.
6. Family backgrounds.
7. Social and cultural differences.
8. Leadership and submission in the home.
9. Attitudes toward sex.
10. Development of a oneness in spirit.
11. Growth after marriage.
12. Relationship to friends and relatives after marriage.
13. Spiritual matters (assurance of salvation, private and family devotions, regular attendance together in church services, same faith, tithe, etc.).
14. Emotional maturity.
15. Self-esteem of each.
16. Love, marriage, sex, divorce in the Bible.
17. God's will concerning your marriage.
18. The goals, dreams, purposes, and meaning in life of each of you.
19. His special calling in relation to your desires.
20. The role of each.
21. The needs of each of you and how to meet them.

II. PROJECTS DURING ENGAGEMENT

1. Read together and discuss everything in the Bible on love, marriage, sex, resolving conflicts, divorce, submission, headship.
2. Read together and discuss several Christian books on marriage and the home. This is a good way to get to know how the other one feels about important things. Begin with these:

Before You Marry—a workbook by Allan Peterson and
Joyce Smith.
Youth's Marriage Problems—Alfred L. Murray.
(Note especially two chapters: "Problems to Solve
Before Marriage" and "The Engagement Period").
Two to Get Ready—Anthony Florio.
Me? Obey Him?—Mrs. Walt Handford.
3. Read separately some good Christian books on sex:
Life and Love—Clyde Narramore.
The Dating Game and *Sexual Happiness Before Marriage*
—Herbert J. Miles.
The Act of Marriage—Mr. and Mrs. Tim LaHaye.
These should not be constantly on your mind or discussed. They
are helpful in showing the proper Christian attitude toward Christian sex. Perhaps the last two books should be studied just a few
weeks before marriage.
4. Begin a personal improvement program to become the best Christian you possibly can. Become more like Christ daily. He should
also be a growing Christian.
5. Prepare for marriage spiritually, emotionally, physically,
educationally, domestically, socially, financially.
6. Develop the oneness of spirit that is absolutely necessary for a
happy marriage.
7. Study the other person. Know him and his needs. Listen to him.
Encourage (do not nag) him to share himself with you. Share
yourself with him. Talk much to each other.
8. Develop an interest in the things he is interested in. He should do
the same for you. Get involved in many activities together.
9. Attend family conferences. Go together to a Christian marriage
counselor. Get all the help you can. Beware of the person who
feels that he "needs no help"!
10. Work on the proper self-esteem for each of you.

CONCLUSION:

You may ask, "Do we have to agree on everything? If my fiance is not
all you suggested, should we break up?" No, but you should be able to
talk calmly about these things and many other matters without embar-
rassment because of your love for him and because of your desire to meet
his needs. He should be able to do the same. You are not to be carbon
copies. There are male and female differences. There are personality differences. Your very uniqueness is important. The uniqueness of each of
you will affect each other at times. Can you accept this and cope with it?
Are you able to face certain conflicts in an objective, Christian manner,

or do you avoid facing the conflicts, thus causing them to harm the relationship? You will not always agree on everything. However, if you find that you cannot now agree on the really important things, this is the time to talk about them and to weigh them to determine whether you can or should continue in the relationship. Know how he feels about the important matters to you. Let him know how you feel about these subjects, as well as how you feel concerning the topics that really are important to him. *Take time* for this. Do not try to discuss more than one important topic at a sitting. Pray much for the Lord's leadership in this. God can help you form the habit of facing conflicts and difficulties together now. This will help you develop an urgent requirement for happy marriage—being good communicable companions.

—Mrs. Douglas Cravens.

QUESTIONS TO ASK YOURSELF ABOUT THE MAN YOU PLAN TO MARRY

A. Spiritual Aspects:
1. Do we have the same spiritual ideals and habits?
2. If I feel called to a particular ministry, does he share this? If he feels called, do I?
3. Are we comfortable in talking about spiritual matters and in praying together?
4. Do I sense that I have been strengthened spiritually by being with him?
5. Do I have peace in my heart when I pray about God's will regarding him?
6. Does our love meet the standards set in I Corinthians 13?

B. Physical Aspects:
1. Am I proud of the way he looks? (Not just natural good looks, but grooming, posture, etc.)
2. Is there a desire to be close to him?
3. Does he respect me enough to wait for the proper time for showing affection or does he demand immediate gratification? Can we both exercise self-control in this regard?
4. Do we both have the same outlook on purity and the purpose of marriage?

C. Emotional and Mental Aspects:
1. What kind of impression does he make on his employer?
2. Is he considered reliable by others?

3. Does he treat me with courtesy and respect?
4. What makes him angry? How does he react to frustration?
5. Is he often depressed? Do I have to work at building him up continually?
6. Does he have a good reputation about financial matters, paying debts, using money wisely, saving for long-term projects?
7. Do we enjoy many of the same things?
8. Are our educational and intellectual backgrounds similar?

D. Other Aspects:
1. What do I know of his family background? (spiritual, emotional, economic, cultural, etc.).
2. Can I picture him as the father of my children?
3. What kind of relationship does he have with his parents?
4. Do I enjoy being with him, no matter what we are doing?
5. Does my family respond favorably to him? Does our relationship have the blessing of our parents?
6. Does he like my family? Do I like his?
7. What kind of friends does he have?
8. Can I recognize certain weaknesses and differences without attempting to change him?

—Mrs. Joy Martin

NOTE: Mrs. Joy Martin (wife of Dr. Roger Martin) teaches the very popular class for Pastors' Wives at Tennessee Temple Schools. Incidentally, she is my "littlest" sister!

THE WEDDING: HOW THE BRIDE PREPARES

1. Announcements of engagement should be sent to your hometown paper and your fiance's. Indicate date to appear. You may send along an 8 x 10 glossy photo with caption attached.

FOUR TO TWELVE MONTHS BEFORE THE WEDDING:
1. Plan budget within your means; determine where wedding is to be.
2. Visit minister with groom and set date.
3. Choose attendants and invite.
4. Draw up invitation list with groom.
5. Choose a bridal consultant; select dress and attendant's dresses.
6. Select a photographer.
7. See your florist.
8. Plan music.
9. Discuss home and furnishings with fiance. Choose colors.

THREE MONTHS BEFORE WEDDING:
1. Order invitations, stationery, and note paper.
2. Make plans for honeymoon.
3. Shop for trousseau.
4. Have both mothers choose gowns.
5. Visit doctor. Check on rubella immunization.

TWO MONTHS BEFORE WEDDING.
1. Plan recording and display of wedding gifts.
2. Finish addressing wedding invitations.
3. Choose gifts for attendants.
4. Select wedding ring if you have not done so.
5. Go with your fiance to get marriage license.

ONE MONTH BEFORE THE WEDDING:
1. Have your hair styled as you will wear it for wedding.
2. Make transportation plans for wedding party.
3. Final fitting for gown, and for bridesmaids.
4. Order wedding cake.
5. Arrange for rehearsal dinner.
5. Plan accommodations for out-of-town guests.
6. Mail invitations.
7. Prepare newspaper account of wedding.

TWO WEEKS BEFORE THE WEDDING:
1. Record each gift as received.
2. Check on attire for everyone in wedding party.
3. Arrange seating plan for church and reception.
4. Go over personal trousseau.
5. Send typed announcement and glossy photo to newspaper.
6. Arrange for name change on social security, etc.
7. Arrange to move belongings to your new home.

ONE WEEK BEFORE:
1. Have final consultations with caterer, photographer, florist.
2. Have hair done.
3. Plan rehearsal and inform attendants.
4. Get some extra sleep.
5. Take your mother out to lunch and thank her for all she has done for you through the years.

THE WEDDING: HOW THE BRIDEGROOM PREPARES

1. Buy engagement ring.
2. Draw up wedding guest list and check with family.
3. Invite friends to be best man and ushers.
4. Choose formal wear for yourself and attendants, with bride.
5. Choose gifts for best man and ushers, to be given at rehearsal dinner.
6. Choose bride's present—something personal such as jewelry.
7. Select the wedding rings. Should be engraved on inside: C.W.R. to A.N.C., for example, and date.
8. Plan the honeymoon with bride, getting reservations early.
9. Make arrangements to pay for bride's bouquet and mothers' flowers as well as boutonnieres.
10. Get the marriage license. Check state rules about time required. Give to best man the day of wedding.
11. Make sure you have all necessary papers, blood tests, birth certificates, etc. Check about changes in all insurance, including health.
12. Notify your attendants of the hour and place of wedding rehearsal. Give clergyman's fee to best man the day of the wedding (in an envelope, generally $10 to $50 or more).
13. Be sure you and your bride sign the wedding certificate and see that it is safely put away before leaving on your honeymoon.
14. Send a thank you telegram to your bride's parents the next day saying how lovely the wedding and reception were.

THE BEST MAN SHOULD:

1. Take charge of the ushers; brief them on special seating.
2. Get the wedding ring and guard it with your life!
3. Have marriage license and minister's fee ready the day of wedding.
4. Help the groom get ready, making sure his bags are packed; take all bride and groom's luggage to car used for honeymoon.
5. Make sure all tickets and reservations are in groom's pocket after he has changed clothes. Help couple get away.

THE WEDDING: WHO PAYS FOR WHAT?

THE BRIDE PAYS FOR:
1. Wedding ring for the groom if it is a double ring ceremony.
2. Wedding gift for the groom.
3. Presents for the attendants.
4. Accommodations for her attendants from out of town.

5. Personal stationery.
6. Her medical examination.

THE GROOM PAYS FOR:
1. Marriage license.
2. His medical examination.
3. The bride's engagement and wedding rings.
4. Gift for the bride.
5. Bride's bouquet and going-away corsage.
6. Boutonnieres for the men of the wedding party.
7. Flowers for the two mothers.
8. Gloves, ascots, or ties for the men of the wedding party.
9. Gifts for ushers and best man.
10. Accommodations for best man and ushers.
11. Fee for the clergyman.
12. The wedding trip.

THE BRIDE'S FAMILY PAYS FOR:
1. Bride's wedding attire.
2. Wedding invitations.
3. Announcements.
4. Engagement and wedding photographs.
5. Rental for church, if any.
6. Fees for organist, soloist, and janitor.
7. Aisle carpet and canopy.
8. Flowers for the church.
9. Bridesmaids' bouquets.
10. Transportation for bridal party from house to church and reception.
11. Rehearsal dinner (groom's family may choose to pay).
12. Entire cost of reception.

THE GROOM'S FAMILY PAYS FOR:
1. Clothes for the wedding.
2. Any traveling expenses and hotel bills for themselves.
3. Wedding gift for the couple.
4. Optional: rehearsal dinner.

THE ATTENDANTS PAY FOR:
1. Their wedding clothes.
2. Any traveling expenses incurred for themselves.
3. Wedding gift for the couple.

THE GUESTS PAY FOR:
1. Any traveling expenses and hotel bills for themselves.
2. Wedding gifts to the couple.

A CHECK LIST FOR THE CHRISTIAN BRIDE

Planning a wedding, particularly if it is a church wedding, is happy work for a bride but it does involve a careful making of choices and working out of details. While every Christian bride ought to be careful about asking for too many extras that will be hard on the family budget, it is proper and right to attach ceremony and importance to the occasion. Statistics indicate that traditional weddings, performed in church, with a sizable number of invited guests have a better record of stability and longevity than "quickie" weddings performed in the offices of judges or in nontraditional settings, with only a few witnesses.

The spring women's magazines and bride's books nearly always include check lists to help the bride determine such important matters as when to mail out invitations, who pays for the flowers, and the responsibilities of the maid-of-honor, etc. Such lists can be very helpful in organizing the physical details of such an important event.

But there is another check list every bride-to-be ought to go through many weeks before the wedding takes place, and one which is far more important than that which involves gifts, showers, wedding dresses or flowers. In fact, no Christian girl should even allow herself to be committed to any man until she has gone through a spiritual check-up of herself, the man she loves, and the relationship they will have together as man and wife.

The following list of questions is certainly not complete but it should help every Christian girl in determining what she will do with her life and how successful her marriage will be:

1. Do I know, beyond any shadow of doubt, that the man I love has a clear testimony of his faith in Jesus Christ as Saviour? Is he walking in obedience to God's Word, faithful in the house of God, known for his strong witness among his friends and acquaintances? Does he know and love the Word of God?

2. Do I feel confident that he will take the spiritual leadership in the home? Is his relationship with the Lord day by day stable and happy?

3. Am I really committed to the fact that marriage is, in the eyes of God, "until death do us part. . ." without even the slightest consideration of any other alternative?

4. Have I faced the fact that genuine love is not merely a romantic, emotional response in the heat of passion but that it includes a deliberate

continuance of concern and tenderness even in the dark, difficult days when all my romantic feelings may be subdued by pressures of poverty or sickness or tiredness or hard work?

5. Am I committed to the wifely submission taught in Ephesians 5 and I Peter 3? Can I be submissive even when I think I am right, or when I do not understand the reason for my husband's demands? Am I willing to practice a cheerful attitude of submission as well as a daily performance of my husband's wishes and desires?

6. Am I willing to joyfully follow God's leading in the life of my husband, to go, wholeheartedly, wherever God calls him, to do everything in my power to contribute to his ministry and to encourage his service for the Lord?

7. Have I asked God to make me the best possible wife and mother I can be? Can I honestly say that I find joy in the prospect of giving myself completely to satisfy the needs of my husband—physical, social, emotional and spiritual?

8. Do I know, beyond a doubt, that this man is God's best choice for me? Would I be willing to give him up—perhaps never to marry—should God indicate this was not His will for me?

9. Have I accepted the fact that I cannot change this man; that I am marrying him for what he is now, not for what I hope he will become?

10. Have I come to the point where I can say, honestly and sincerely: "Lord, I am yours; this man I love is yours, and this marriage is yours. I now acknowledge your right to do with us anything that will bring glory and honor to your name. Amen"?

There is no peace on earth today save the peace in the heart
At home with God. From that sure habitation
The heart looks forth upon the sorrows of the savage world
And pities them, and ministers to them; but is not impli-
    cated.
All else has failed, as it must always fail.
No man can be at peace with his neighbor who is not at peace
With himself; the troubled mind is a troublemaker.

—Edna St. Vincents Milay
from "Conversation at Midnight"

Husbands First of All!

I'm free, THE MOVEMENT says.
I can be whatever I want to be.
I don't have to spend my life
   mopping up spilled milk,
   getting out ring-around-the collar,
   hunting for lost cufflinks,
   matching up socks—or even
   scratching somebody's back.
I can write the great American novel
Or hawk my macrame plant holders
   at the craft festivals
   (wearing a gypsy scarf on my head,
   and dirty tennis shoes on my feet—
   or maybe no shoes at all).
I can be a lady executive
   and try not to worry about whether
   I took the roast out of the freezer
   (THE MOVEMENT wouldn't like that!)
   Or I could run for Congress—
   (That can't be much harder than
   presiding over the PTA
     Or figuring out my own income tax
      Or brilliantly coordinating my
      returnable pop bottles
      and newspaper coupons
   to buy 53 dollars' worth of groceries
   with only 48 dollars and 26 cents.)
So I'm free, am I?
Then I choose. . .I choose
   the "promise to obey" part of the marriage vows,
   the nose-wiping of a two-year-old,
   the bargainings with my teenagers to use—
     the car
     the typewriter
     the telephone
     the bathroom.
I choose the endless procession of
     bag lunches
     peanut butter sandwiches
     dirty dog dishes
     potato chip crumbs
      and yesterday's newspaper.

I choose the warm curve of your back on a cold night,
    the precarious pleasure of an empty bank account
      when all the bills are paid,
    the promises of European tours
      when the children finish college.
I choose to make your toast (dark) and your
    eggs (easy over).
I choose to listen for your car turn in the drive
I choose to nudge you when you snore.
No matter what THE MOVEMENT SAYS: I choose you!

                        —Jessie Sandberg.

WHAT IS A HUSBAND?

When a boy lays aside his tops, his marbles, and his bike in favor of a girl, another girl, and still another girl, he becomes a youth. When the youth discards his first girl and his second girl for *the* girl, he becomes a bachelor. And when the bachelor can stand it no longer, he turns into a husband.

A husband does not collect tops, marbles, or bikes. Not that he wouldn't like to collect such things again; it's just that he is so busy collecting money, shoes, groceries, rent receipts, automobile parts, faucet handles, and fillings in his teeth, as well as trying to keep people from cleaning up his workshop or his study, that he simply hasn't time for the luxuries of life.

A new husband, all dreamy-eyed. . .confidently believes he has married a girl. Poor fellow! Let us not disturb him. . .for too soon will he discover he has married a master of tactical warfare, a financial wizard, a mind reader, an inventor, a Rock of Gibraltar, a judge, jury, and prosecuting attorney. In addition to a wife, he has acquired an oracle, siren, kitten. . .a beautiful, illogical, single-purposed female.

Husbands come in all sizes—small, medium, large, and the giant economy package with the 42-inch waist. Some are rich and others are poor, but mostly a husband is somewhere just a little back of the middle, and if nothing happens between now and next payday, he ought to be running pretty well up in the pack. But something *always* happens. He has forgotten about the taxes or the insurance. Or how was he to know that *the* girl was going to back the car through the garage door?

A husband is the handiest thing invented. How else would a wife get the furniture moved, the phone company bawled out, the dresser drawer unstuck, the finance company reasoned with, her zipper fixed, her back rubbed, her supper praised, or the tip of her nose kissed?

Who but a husband could unjitter her nerves, take kitty to the vet, stand on the tiptop of the ladder, get the lids off pickle jars, put up the bed when Aunt Hattie comes, be a handsome escort, hold her hand when the world starts to black out, laugh in the face of disaster, and keep her feet warm in winter?

Husbands like ball games. . .camping out. . sports cars. . .man size dogs. . .machinery that can be taken apart. . .very old clothes. . . boats. . .golf clubs. . .and coming home every night to *the* girl. . .

A husband is happiest when he is taking something apart. . .slowest when supper is on the table getting cold; fastest when the light turns green; maddest when somebody has used his razor again; tiredest when *the* girl is the liveliest. . . .

Husbands can take a tire off a rim, lift a sofa into an attic, or stretch a $10 bill until Friday, but they become as putty when confronted by a woman in tears, be she age one, ten, or one hundred and ten.

A husband is a cheerful, patient, hard-working guy who never quite caught up with his dreams. Maybe he is not so handsome and trim as he was on that certain day long ago; maybe he is a little bald on top, a bit more tired at night; but he is still the only person in the world who can make things right when he holds you in his arms and says those old familiar words.

What is a husband? He is the one who, with a touch, can bring back the starlight and glow of years long ago. At least he hopes he can—don't disappoint him.

—Alan Beck (Revised).

BE NOT DECEIVED

Be not deceived because my tongue is mute,
Still as a broken string upon a lute,
Silenced by stubborn pride that is too strong
To own that you are right and I am wrong.
I have compounded error with the fault
Of cruel words my reason could not halt.
And now stiff-necked I stand. Be not deceived
By this dumb tongue. I am ashamed and grieved
And I would say my bitter tongue has lied,
Were I not crippled by ignoble pride.
Be not, my love—be not deceived because

No words rush out to purge my grievous flaws.
My hands beseech the love my tongue denies,
And you can see the pleading in my eyes.
          —Georgie Starbuck Galbraith in *Good Housekeeping.*

WHAT IS MATURITY?

Maturity is the ability to control anger and settle differences without violence or destruction.

Maturity is patience. It is the willingness to pass up immediate pleasure in favor of the long-term gain.

Maturity is perseverance, the ability to sweat out a project or a situation in spite of heavy opposition and discouraging setbacks.

Maturity is the capacity to face unpleasantness and frustration, discomfort and defeat, without complaint or collapse.

Maturity is humility. It is being big enough to say, "I was wrong." And, when right, the mature person need not experience the satisfaction of saying, "I told you so."

Maturity is the ability to make a decision and stand by it. The immature spend their lives exploring endless possibilities; then they do nothing.

Maturity means dependability, keeping one's word, coming through in a crisis. The immature are masters of the alibi. They are the confused and the disorganized. Their lives are "mazes of broken promises, former friends, unfinished business and good intentions that somehow never materialize."

Maturity is the art of living in peace with that which we cannot change, the courage to change that which SHOULD be changed—and the wisdom to know the difference.

NOTE: The original source of this is unknown but it has appeared several times in Ann Landers' newspaper column.

POSSESSIONS

"To be without some of the things you want is an indispensable part of happiness."

          —Bertrand Russell

A WOMAN'S SUBMISSION:
What Does It Really Mean?

One of the most difficult problems that an earnest Christian wife has to face is that which involves the "how to" of fulfilling the biblical command of submission, especially to her own husband. No matter what arguments the Women's Lib Movement may present for action to the contrary; no matter what power a woman may possess legally, the biblical command is clear:

"Wives, submit yourselves unto your own husbands, as unto the Lord. For the husband is the head of the wife, even as Christ is the head of the church: and he is the saviour of the body. Therefore as the church is subject unto Christ, so let the wives be to their own husbands in every thing."—Eph. 5:22-24.

Some wife who is angry and resentful about accepting such a principle is apt to point out that the same passage commands husbands to "love their wives as their own bodies" (vs. 28), and to cite cases in which Christian men have failed to fulfill this scriptural command. She thereby suggests that a man's disobedience nullifies a woman's responsibility to follow what the Scripture commands.

Such thinking is not only wrong and damaging; it is foolish and illogical as well. In our government, we have laws which state that driving above a posted speed limit is an offence which is punishable by fine and, in some special cases, by imprisonment. Not every driver who exceeds the speed limit is caught and not every driver who is caught is punished. But whether or not someone else breaks speed laws; whether or not he appears to get away with it—I am still subject to the law. It would be dangerous and wrong for me to assume that the law is null and void for me simply because someone else broke it.

There is, however, a blessed and wonderful law of sowing and reaping in the Scripture which is applicable at this point, I feel. A cheerful obedience to the Scripture on the part of one person tends to encourage obedience on the part of others, and in no situation is this more true than in marriage. Submission encourages love; love encourages submission.

In the book, *Adolescent Behavior and Development*, the author states the relationship between submission and love in a good marriage:

True intimacy is a condition of total trust in another person, coupled with close affection or love for him; and it cannot be attained without surrender of autonomy. Paradoxically, autonomy cannot be soundly maintained without intimacy. . . .

A woman who sets out to fulfill her spiritual and practical responsibilities as a wife, claiming the power of the Holy Spirit, and keeping a sense of balance and self-esteem in the process can develop a climate in the home which will encourage the best possible relationship with her husband in the home. Dr. Marie Robinson says about this kind of spiritual love:

In work, in play, in all the inner and outer activities of life, the individual (loved) becomes far more vital and productive than before. . . .In love we never encounter a man trampling on his wife's rights and needs, or a woman competing with her husband. The value of the other as he is and as he can grow to be, becomes the highest value in life.

Now the question arises: "Fine, I accept the biblical command; but how can I apply it in the little day-by-day problems of my own marriage?"

Let's consider the following principles regarding submission:

1. Biblical submission is not synonymous with spinelessness, lack of character or conviction, lack of spiritual initiative and enthusiasm, or a failure to establish specific personal goals. When the Scripture praises the womanly virtue of a "meek and quiet spirit, which is in the sight of God of great price" (I Pet. 3:4), there is not the slightest suggestion indicated that this means a shrugging of the shoulder when there are wrongs to be righted, where there are standards to be upheld.

No Christian woman can be the kind of citizen she ought to be if she has no concern for the national issues that concern her family, and sometimes she ought to take a stand in the school and community on moral issues that will have an effect on the spiritual development of her own children.

Not long ago a young woman asked me, "How can I use the authority and force to discipline and control my children if I am constantly practicing submission to my husband? Somehow, it doesn't seem that the two could be compatible."

My answer to that problem is that authority is not something we take upon ourselves; it is something which is delegated to us by God. Since God did not give me authority over my husband, I dare not take it into my own hands. However, God *has* delegated authority to the mother just as he has given authority to the father ("Honour thy father *and thy mother*. . ." (Exod. 20:12), and so a responsible Christian mother must remember that when she demands obedience and righteousness from her children, she is acting on the authority of God Himself.

No Christian woman can be the kind of mother she ought to be without the holy courage to rear her children according to biblical standards. No matter how strong a father's convictions may be about rearing children according to the Bible, it is the mother who generally spends the greatest amount of time with children when they are small, and it is she who will have to determine to train them as they ought to be trained.

Even aside from the matter of children, a Christian woman ought to have some goals and ambitions for her own life. She ought to earnestly seek to find ways to use for His glory all the gifts and abilities which God has given her. She ought to long to be a soul winner. She ought to be interested and enthusiastic about the things going on around her. She ought to be concerned for the needs of other people. She ought to have respect and care for her own body, not only for the sake of her husband but because she is an important person in the eyes of God. If these characteristics were not compatible with the biblical view of submission, then God would not have given us so careful a description of the virtuous woman in Proverbs 31. This intelligent and busy woman was an excellent homemaker, boss, businesswoman, mother, wife and neighbor, and the description of her is concluded with these words: "Her children arise up, and call her blessed; her husband also, and he praiseth her."

2. Biblical submission *is* for a Christian woman to genuinely desire to please her husband and to make him happy—not merely to obey in the coldest calculation of what is required but to work at developing a sensitivity and insight regarding his needs. It is true of our relationship to the Lord that our attitude is what really establishes our behavior and surely this is true of marriage as well. When we long to please the one we love, then our actions will follow suite.

Robert Zack isn't too far from the truth when he says:

> How absurd a heart can be!
> When it's bound, it feels most free.
> When it's free it wanders 'round
> Seeking so it can be bound.
> All this simply means to me
> Words do not say as they sound—
> Freedom's not 'til love is found!

3. Biblical submission is not simply agreeing to the word "obey" in the marriage vows. In fact, it is not even a matter which one settles in a once-for-all decision. It involves a day-by-day, hour-by-hour giving up of one's rights in practical, individual matters. A submissive heart is one which is developed through the years with practice, patience and the power of the Holy Spirit.

4. Biblical submission is an attitude before it is an act. Psalm 40:8 is a verse that should be memorized and practiced by every Christian wife: "I *delight* to do thy will, O my God: yea, thy law is within my heart." We will not be able to make submission work in our homes until we are able to say, "I *want* to be a submissive wife, Lord. Teach me how to make it practical in my life."

5. Biblical submission involves complete confidence that God's will is the very best for me. One great saint of God said: "I can leave with God all the consequences of complete obedience to His will." I don't need to

be caught up in all kinds of speculations about, "What if. . . ?" My responsibility is simply to obey His Word.

6. Biblical submission is unconditional. It has nothing to do with one's greater or lesser intelligence or maturity or competence. It is an act based entirely on the command of God.

7. Biblical submission is not nullified by a wife's spiritual superiority to her husband. The better Christian woman I am, the more spiritually-minded I am, the more gifts of leadership I possess, the easier it ought to be for me to submit to those God has put in authority over me.

Dorothy Enslin, a secular writer with unusual insight in the personal relationships of the home, says:

> . . .Let woman take man as he comes home rather worse for wear. . . Take him, woman, as you promised, to have and to hold, for better and for worse. Fondly, as Pygmalion molded Galatia, restore his manhood. . .A woman who reneges on her marriage contract blights her own dream. Marriage is not a defunct trade like quilting or horse-shoeing. . .If she can keep her children and her husband loving their home, if she can tune herself to their changing needs, she is building an astral bank account that pays in interest compounded daily.

8. Biblical submission is intelligent and voluntary. It is not simply "putting up" with something which someone else requires of me but a deliberate giving of myself to the place God has ordained for me.

9. Biblical submission requires prayer: "Give me wisdom to know how to lean on my husband just as I submit to God and lean on Him." "But I would have you know, that the head of every man is Christ; and the head of the woman is the man; and the head of Christ is God" (I Cor. 11:3).

10. Refusal to submit to the authority of my husband is a failure in understanding myself and my own needs. God does not design any of His creatures to function a particular way without giving that creation the qualities needed to fulfill that given role: Following God's plan for my life will make me happier as a person and as a woman.

Refusal to submit to the authority of my husband expresses a lack of faith in the Lord to do right. Jeremiah 29:11 says: "For I know the thoughts that I think toward you, saith the Lord, thoughts of peace and not of evil, to give you an expected end." God's plans for those He loves are always to make us happy. He does not fail in His promises toward those who set out to follow His Word.

"Nothing lies beyond the reach of prayer but that which lies beyond the will of God."

—R. A. Torrey

LOVE'S EYES

Love gave me eyes that could behold
Your special worth of purest gold,
Your beauty shining like a star,
And all the splendid things you are:
Your honor and your tenderness,
The willing heart with which you bless
The small and helpless, and your hands
That compass what your will demands.
I see you good as you are kind,
And know full well love is not blind,
Disclosing what I hold so dearly,
It only makes me see more clearly.
—Georgie Starbuck Galbraith.

MONEY IN MARRIAGE
By Mr. John Economidis

A guide for periodically reviewing your family finances to help prevent the disagreements that, family counselors tell us, often lead to serious marital difficulties.

YES NO

( ) ( ) We save part of each paycheck, even if it is a small part.

( ) ( ) We keep a written record of our monthly expenses.

( ) ( ) If we feel we have not allowed ourselves enough money to spend for things we'd enjoy (e.g., personal luxuries, travel), we will carefully evaluate whether we are spending more in another category (e.g., hobbies, entertainment) than we want to or have to. No spending, whether it be big payments as for housing or insurance, or smaller ones, as for interest on a loan or a night out, is exempt from such evaluation.

( ) ( ) If we decided, last time we talked about our finances, to cut our spending in any category, we accomplished this goal.

( ) ( ) We have not ignored small money problems but have handled them as they arose. We know that ignored, unresolved problems can lead to greater problems and to quarrels.

( ) ( ) One or both of us balances our bank statement with our checkbook when the statement arrives.

( ) ( ) We pay all of our bills promptly to protect our credit rating.

( ) ( ) If we feel we have been spending too much cash out of our wallets, we each will start the day carrying only a specified, limited amount of cash.

( ) ( ) Neither of us has used money or the things it buys, in place of more personal means, to display affection for each other or our children.

( ) ( ) Neither of us has used personal income to make himself or herself feel more significant, important, competent, self-reliant, or independent.

( ) ( ) If one of us occasionally does something contrary to our mutual financial goals, the other does not try to "get even." When one of us resists an impulse to abandon our financial plan, the other praises him or her.

( ) ( ) Neither of us deprives the other of basic necessities by trying to save an unreasonable amount of money.

( ) ( ) Before we shop for a product or service, we inform ourselves about it as thoroughly as we can.

( ) ( ) Neither of us indulges in an expensive activity, hobby, or possession unless the other agrees to the expenditure.

(Credit for the above is given to: *The Family Banker,* "Your Guide to Better Money Management.")

*HOW MUCH DEBT CAN
    YOU AFFORD?*

MONTHLY INCOME

Take-Home Pay _____

Other Income _____

Total Income _____

**MONTHLY EXPENSES
(FIXED)**

Mortage or Rent _____

Life Insurance _____

Auto Insurance _____

Local Taxes _____

**MONTHLY EXPENSES
(VARIABLE)**

Utilities _____

Medical (Inc. Med. Ins.) _____

1. Enter your TAKE-HOME pay plus any steady outside income.

2. List all monthly living costs in the "Monthly Expenses" (fixed) or (variable). Estimate the variable costs as closely as possible.

3. Deduct total reduced expenses from the total income figure. The remainder represents the MAXIMUM that you can afford each month for debt payments.

4. To check whether you are operating within a safe debt-payment limit, figure your present debt load in the bottom section of the form. If you want to use the 12-month safety rule, the total amount LEFT TO PAY should NOT exceed 12 times your MONTHLY INSTALLMENTS total.

Food   ————
Clothing   ————
Recreation   ————
Furnishing and Other
  Household Exp.   ————
Saving, Investments ————
Other   ————
TOTAL EXPENSES ————
TOTAL INCOME
  (From above) ————
  Minus
TOTAL EXPENSES
  (From above) ————
Your Monthly Debt-
  Payment Limit ————

5. Another way to test whether you are using credit too liberally is as follows: The total MONTHY INSTALLMENTS figure should be around 15% of the TOTAL INCOME figure.
6. You should note that NO PROVISION has been made from "Monthly Income" for the TITHE which belongs to the Lord. THIS SHOULD BE TAKEN INTO CONSIDERATION WHEN FIGURING YOUR "MONTHLY DEBT-PAYMENT LIMIT."

* * * * *

The following data concern the expenditures of the average American family in the U. S. This information was published by the Bureau of Labor. Compare how your family spends.

Food 24%
Rent or Mortgage 24%
Household appliances 5%
Shoes and clothes 10%
Auto Expenses 15%

Med. Ins., Doctor bills, drugs plus personal care such as haircuts, cosmetics, beauty parlor 9%
Savings 5%
Recreation 4%
Education 4%

HOME POEM

Where love finds a place,
Beautiful things are. . .
Like going upstairs together,
Like going down alone in the night barefoot to query the lock.
Like watching the weather
    Rain stinging the windows
    Snow clinging to the panes
    Wind singing.
    (Love is lovely when it rains.)

Like sitting across from each other
    and not being cross.
Like not getting up in the morning.
    No loss!
    (Except time's little cry from the clock.)
Like his finding her earring
    And her finding his sock.
It's a total of both tied up in a bundle of walls.
An echo chamber of selves connected by halls.

                                 —Maxine Lewis.

"WITH THIS RING I THEE WED. . ."

I think it is about time somebody stood up and gave three cheers for marriage! The world is doing a lot of talking these days about the pleasures of being a "swinging single." In fact, a whole cult is building up in our country around this idea. There are now "singles bars," singles apartment buildings, singles clubs, and the advertising world is cashing in by promoting cosmetics, sports gear, clothes, vacations and restaurants designed especially for this group.

I am well aware of the fact that God did not intend every person to marry. I know dozens of women who live busy, fruitful lives without a family. Some, I think, have even chosen singleness as a way of life for the cause of Christ. Perhaps they had opportunities to marry but felt their opportunities for service for the Lord would be increased alone. Others, no doubt, would have married had the Lord led them to the right man, but have found a life of contentment and joy outside of marriage.

God bless all of these dear women!

What concerns me is the trend in our time to avoid commitments and obligations that come with marriage and the rearing of a family. I am alarmed at the casual attitude even many Christians have toward the common practice of young people living together without benefit of the marriage ceremony. No matter what the Women's Movement may say, a woman who tries to avoid the responsibilities and involvement of a home and family simply because she does not want to be tied down and committed to a life of service for others, is cheating herself.

We forget that marriage is an institution created by God—the first institution, in fact—and it is of more significance than any other human institution, including government and the church. God knew what men and women would need to be most fulfilled, to function most efficiently, to be happiest and safest in a world endangered and contaminated by sin. Marriage enables two people to build a relationship—physical, spiritual and emotional—so unique and intimate and holy that God could make it a beautiful picture of Jesus Christ's relationship to the church.

In spite of the decay of our contemporary moral condition, the institution of marriage is still a precious gift of God to mankind. How important it is that every child of God do everything possible to preserve a standard of righteousness for his own marriage, to determine that nothing will damage the sanctity and quality of the home!

And how important it is that we teach our children the beauty and holiness of marriage, not only by example but by careful teaching from the Word of God. How sad it is that we provide a college education, we teach them to drive a car, to handle money, to develop other skills, but we neglect this most important training of all—how to have the right kind of marriage.

Thank God for marriage! May we seek for a renewal of God's blessing on the Christian home.

"God setteth the solitary in families. . . ."—Ps. 68:6.

"Therefore shall a man leave his father and his mother, and shall cleave unto his wife: and they shall be one flesh."—Gen. 2:24.

"Wives, submit yourselves unto your own husbands, as unto the Lord. For the husband is head of the wife, even as Christ is the head of the church: and he is the saviour of the body. Therefore as the church is subject unto Christ, so let the wives be to their own husbands in every thing. Husbands, love your wives even as Christ also loved the church, and gave himself for it; That he might sanctify and cleanse it with the washing of the water by the word, That he might present it to himself a glorious church, not having spot, or wrinkle, or any such thing; but that it should be holy and without blemish. . . ."—Eph. 5:22-27.

I'M CARED FOR

(A wife's tribute to her husband)

Lot's of things around my home tell me that I'm cared for.

Lush, green grass—freshly mowed,
 A willing arm to bear my heavy load.
Gas tank in *my* car always filled,
Discovering my garden had already been tilled.
Lights replaced without ado,

Breakfast fixed each Saturday, too!
Walls repapered without complaint,
   Hallways with their *washable* paint.
Pictures hung eyelevel (and sometimes below).
   All because I want them so.
Fun surprises in boxes and bags,
   Sometimes hidden for me to find.
   Evidence that time was spent with ME in mind.
Invitations to MacDonald's with the kids,
   When it's obvious I've been worn to a frizz.
Dinner dates with the most precious sweetheart around,
   Those private, quiet, uninterrupted talks,
   Secret smiles, hand held securely,
   Gentle encouragements, sweet words of love abound.
Knees bent in prayer at the end of the day,
   Asking the Lord to guide my way.

Fifteen years used to seem so much—
   But Dear, they've flown by as if a touch.
Thank you for all these things and more,
Things that tell me. . .
        I'M CARED FOR.

                        —Mrs. Alden Guy.
                       Used by permission.

We are not here to dream, to drift;
There is hard work to do and loads to lift;
Shun not the struggle—face it—'tis God's gift. Be strong!
It matters not how deep entrenched the wrong,
How hard the battle goes, the day how long;
Faint not! Fight on! Tomorrow comes the song.
                     —M. Babcock

    Great vices and great virtues are an accumulation of small ones.

Practical Helps

IDEAS FOR SAVING VITAMINS
AND OTHER NUTRIENTS

1. Cook vegetables in as little water as possible. Save vegetable water for soups and gravies.
2. Cook fresh vegetables only until tender. Extended cooking destroys nutrients.
3. Heat canned vegetables only to serving temperature. Do not boil.
4. Do not peel vegetables until just before cooking.
5. Add the tender tops of root vegetables (as well as celery tops) to salads. These are rich in vitamin A.
6. Eat potatoes with the skin as much as possible. Leave skin on even when making french fries.
7. Keep frozen foods at 0 or less to keep food at its best nutritive value. Carefully rotate foods in freezer so that you do not store for too long a period. Beef should be used within 1 year, pork within six months, and fish and ground meat within 3 months. All fruits and vegetables should be used within 8 months.
8. Remember that the pulp of oranges and grapefruit have certain nutrients which are lost when only the juice is used.
9. Use evaporated milk and half-and-half in recipes which call for heavy cream (cannot be substituted when cream is to be whipped). These contain more protein and calcium and fewer calories.
10. Bruised fruit results in a loss of vitamins A and C. Cut with a sharp knife.

HOW TO MAKE WHITE SAUCE

Every cook needs to learn how to make a good white sauce since it is a basic part of so many different dishes, specifically, cream soups, creamed vegetables, souffles and croquettes. Here is the basic recipe:

2 TBS. butter or margarine
2 TBS. flour
¼ tsp. salt
1/8 tsp. pepper
1 cup milk

Melt butter or margarine in a medium-sized saucepan and add flour, salt and pepper. Stir with a wooden spoon until smooth. Gradually pour in milk, stirring constantly until sauce comes to boiling. Boil 1 minute

and remove from heat. Makes 1 cup. (Double recipe if needed.)
    Variations:

> *Substitute chicken broth for milk.*
> **Mornay sauce;** *Add 2 TBS. each grated Swiss and Parmesan cheese and stir until melted. Do not boil.*
> **Cheese sauce #1:** *Add ¼ lb. grated Cheddar cheese. Do not boil.*
> **Cheese sauce #2:** *Add ¼ lb. cubed cream cheese. Do not boil.*

NOTE: This recipe has been included at the request of our young cook, Carol, who says: "Nobody ever tells a bride how important it is to know how to make white sauce!"

TIRED OF DOING THINGS THE SAME OLD WAY?

* Serve your children a surprise breakfast of hot dogs and ice cream (more nutrition than most breakfasts!)
* Add sour cream to your mashed potatoes.
* Add chopped peanuts to creamed chipped beef or cheese sauce.
* Serve your family a "finger supper" to be eaten in front of the fireplace: cold meat cubes on toothpicks, fruit, raw vegetable sticks, cheese sticks and crackers.
* Serve sticks of peppermint or lemon candy with cups of hot tea. Guests stir, sweeten and flavor their tea all at once—and no spoons to wash. Peppermint or molasses sticks are wonderful with hot cocoa, too.

HOW TO REMOVE COMMON HOUSEHOLD STAINS FROM FABRIC OR UPHOLSTERY

BLOOD: Sponge with mild detergent solution and cool water.

CANDLE WAX: Chill with an ice cube wrapped in a towel. Scrape with a blunt-edged knife, then use cleaning fluid.

CHEWING GUM: Chill gum with ice cube wrapped in a towel. Scrape without spreading, then apply trichloroethylene fluid. (Risky to use on furniture upholstered with foam padding; not recommended on triacetate or polyester fabrics.) Repeat.

CHOCOLATE: Sponge with mild detergent solution (1 tsp. to 1 cup water). Rinse well. OR: Use spot-lifter as directed on spray can, or cleaning fluid. Test first in inconspicuous spot. Cleaning fluid may attack foam padding of furniture and is not recommended for triacetate or polyester fabrics.

COFFEE (black), TEA: Sponge with mild detergent solution. Rinse well.

COFFEE (milk), TEA: Sponge sparingly with cold water several times. Use spot-lifter as directed on spray can, or cleaning fluid.

CRAYON: Scrape with blunt edge of knife. Use spray-on cleaner, followed, if necessary, by cleaning fluid. (Test first in an inconspicuous spot; flammable; use in a well-ventilated room away from sources of combustion.)

HEAVY GREASE, LIPSTICK, TAR, ASPHALT: Chill with ice cube and scrape, without spreading, with dull knife. Try dry-cleaning fluid (test first) followed by spray rug or upholstery cleaner.

INK (Felt-tip, Ballpoint pens): Questionable. Some will come out with dry-cleaning fluid used sparingly but repeatedly. Some can be removed by spraying with hair spray and then washing out the hair spray with mild detergent solution. May need professional cleaning.

NAIL POLISH: If not on acetate, use nail-polish remover with care; may need professional cleaning.

PAINT (Dry, partially dry): On upholstery, soften mixture with equal parts of alcohol and benzine (flammable). Try turpentine followed by detergent and warm water. (Wet latex and acrylic paints can be removed with water.)

POISON PLANTS TO AVOID

Poison ivy grows in a number of different forms and the color of the leaves changes with the seasons—from purplish to green to pink, red or yellow. However, it always has three leaflets. *Poison oak* is very similar but the leaves appear to be more hairy.

Poison sumac has a series of long narrow leaves arranged opposite one another on a stalk which is red-ribbed. The berries are grayish white and hang down when they are ripe. It is a tall shrub which is more apt to grow in swampy areas.

A little boy was questioned by reporters after his family's house had been destroyed by fire.

"Is it true that your home has burned down, Son?" the reporter asked.

"Oh, no," the little boy replied. "We still have a home. We just don't have a house to put it in."

COMMON FOOD SUBSTITUTES

WHEN THE RECIPE CALLS FOR:	YOU CAN USE:
1 TBS. cornstarch	2 TBS. all-purpose flour
1 whole egg	2 egg yolks plus 1 TBS. water
1 cup homogenized milk	1 cup skim milk plus 2 TBS. butter or margarine OR: ½ cup evaporated milk plus ½ cup water
1 ounce unsweetened chocolate	3 TBS. cocoa plus 1 TBS. butter or margarine
1 tsp. baking powder	½ tsp. cream of tartar plus ¼ tsp. baking soda
1 cup sifted cake flour	7/8 cup sifted all-purpose flour (7/8 cup is 1 cup less 2 TBS.)
½ cup (1 stick) butter or margarine	7 TBS. vegetable shortening
1 cup sour or buttermilk	1 TBS. white vinegar plus sweet milk to equal 1 cup
1 clove fresh garlic	1 tsp. garlic salt OR: 1/8 tsp. garlic powder
2 tsp. minced onion	1 tsp. onion powder
1 TBS. finely chopped fresh chives	1 tsp. freeze-dried chives
1 cup dairy sour cream	1 TBS. lemon juice plus evaporated milk to equal one cup

When You Entertain

THE CORRECT WAY TO SET A TABLE

The primary rule for setting a table, whether formal or informal, is that *silverware* is placed in order of use. In other words, the piece which is placed farthest away from the plate is the piece to be used first. The knife goes on the right side immediately next to the plate, with the blade turned in toward the plate. The dinner fork goes on the left side, immediately next to the plate. If soup is to be served, the soup spoon is placed to the right of the knife. If an appetizer is served requiring a small fork, it will go to the right of the soup spoon. The salad fork goes to the left of the plate, next to the dinner fork. If butter plates are used, the butter knife is placed across the top of the plate, handle to the right, blade pointing inward. Coffee spoons may be placed on the outside, righthand to the plate if coffee is served during the meal, or brought in when the coffee is served. Dessert forks or spoons are brought in with the dessert, or they may be placed above the plate, parallel to the edge of the table.

Napkins should be placed to the left of the plate, edges in toward plate or, if there is no soup or appetizer served, it may be placed on the plate. It is acceptable today to fold napkins in any pleasing manner or to use a variety of napkin rings.

China: The dinner plate is put at the center of the place setting if food is to be passed at the table. If plates are to be served in the kitchen the place is left bare. However, if an appetizer is to be served, it should be put on the table at each plate before the guests are seated. The bread-and-butter plates are directly above the forks. Salad plates go immediately above the dinner plates.

Glasses are placed on the right above the knives. The water glass goes at the point of the dinner knife with glasses serving other cold beverages slightly to the right.

Seating: The host and hostess usually sit at opposite ends of the table with men and women alternating around the table. A special female guest sits to the right of the host and a special male guest sits to the right of the hostess.

Centerpieces should be low enough that guests can see over them and small enough that they do not distract from the rest of the table setting. Don't be afraid to think creatively when planning a centerpiece. While fresh, cut flowers are most commonly used, it is also acceptable to use arrangments of potted plants, bowls of fruits or vegetables, dried flower arrangements or wildflowers and weeds tastefully arranged in varieties of ways. Candles may be either high or low but the flame should not be at the eye level of the guests.

Making do with what you have: If you are having more guests than you have complete dinner service to accommodate, don't be afraid to combine various china pieces or silver. Either alternate place settings or use coffee cups and salad plates from another set. If you collect individual coffee cups and saucers, use a different one for each guest and show them off. If you are lacking particular serving pieces, adapt. Guests who are really enjoying your hospitality will be impressed at your cleverness and originality. Then remember that the way you treat guests in your home is far more important than the things you use to entertain them.

CANDY STRAWBERRIES

2 pkgs. (3 oz. each) strawberry-flavor gelatin
1 cup chopped pecans
1 cup shredded coconut
½ cup sweetened condensed milk (not evaporated)
1 tsp. vanilla extract
Red and green crystallized sugar
Slivered almonds
Green food coloring.

Mix first 5 ingredients together and shape into little strawberries. Roll in red crystallized sugar. Dip tops in green sugar. For stems, dip almonds in green food coloring and insert one in each berry. Makes about 3 dozen.

HORS D'OUVRES PIE

Buy (or make) large round loaves of bread which have not been pre-sliced. You will need to slice these yourself horizontally so that you will have large, round slices shaped like a pie.

Butter each slice and then place various sandwich mixes in rings until bread is covered. You may wish to decorate outside edge with cheese squeezed through a cake decorating tube. Garnish with olives.

Suggested sandwich "mixings":

egg salad

ham salad

softened liver sausage

pimento cheese

tuna salad

cream cheese with nuts and pineapple

Arrange rings of fillings to create the most pleasing arrangement of texture and color.

Cut into pie-shaped wedges and serve.

SAUSAGE-CHEESE APPETIZERS

1 pound mild pork sausage

1 pound medium Cheddar cheese, shredded

3 cups biscuit mix

Crumble sausage into a large bowl; add cheese and mix well. Gradually add biscuit mix blending with hands or a pastry blender. Shape into walnut-size balls and place on an ungreased cookie sheet. Bake at 350°F. for 10-15 minutes. Yields about 9 dozen.

NOTE: After baking, these can be frozen in moisture-proof containers. To serve, remove from freezer and heat at 350° F. until warm.

POPCORN BALLS

2 quarts unsalted popcorn

1 cup light corn syrup

1 tsp. vinegar

2 TBS. butter or margarine

1 tsp. vanilla extract

Four drops red food coloring (optional)

Place popcorn in a large, greased bowl. Combine corn syrup and vinegar in a small saucepan. Boil slowly until a candy thermometer registers 260° F., or a small amount of syrup dropped in cold water forms a hard ball. Remove syrup from heat and stir in butter, vanilla and, if desired, food coloring. Pour syrup over popcorn in bowl and toss with 2 forks until corn is well coated. Cool slightly. Shape into balls of desired size and place on buttered plate. Makes about seven 3-inch balls.

OLD-FASHIONED MOLASSES TAFFY

1 cup unsulfured molasses
1 cup sugar
1 TBS. butter or margarine
Dash of salt

Mix all ingredients in saucepan. Put over low heat and stir until sugar is dissolved. Cook over medium heat until a small amount of mixture separates in hard but not brittle threads when dropped in very cold water (270° F. on a candy thermometer.) Pour onto greased platter. As edges cool, fold toward center. When cool enough to handle, press into ball with lightly buttered fingers. Pull until light in color and very firm. Stretch into a long rope ½" in diameter and cut in 1" pieces. Wrap each piece in waxed paper or plastic wrap. Makes about 1¼ pounds.

SPILLS AND SMELLS

* *To cut unpleasant odor in the kitchen, boil 1 teaspoon of vanilla with a little water.*

* *Remove stain from mattress or upholstery by making thick paste of starch and water. Apply, dry and then vacuum.*

* *Clean garbage disposal: mix 1 cup vinegar with water to fill ice tray. Run cubes through disposal.*

The Sum of Motherhood

TO THE ADOPTED BABY. . .

Not flesh of my flesh
nor bone of my bone
but miraculously my own.
Never forget—even for a minute
you weren't born under my heart
but in it.

— Author unknown.

TWELVE RULES FOR RAISING DELINQUENT CHILDREN

1. Begin with infancy to give the child everything he wants. In this way he will grow up to believe the world owes him a living.
2. When he picks up bad words, laugh at him. This will make him think he's cute. It will also encourage him to pick up "cuter" phrases that will blow off the top of your head later.
3. Never give him any spiritual training. Wait until he is 21 and then let him "decide for himself."
4. Avoid use of the word "wrong." It may develop a guilt complex. This will condition him to believe later, when he is arrested for stealing a car, that society is against him and he is being persecuted.
5. Pick up everything he leaves around—books, shoes and clothes. Do everything for him so that he will be experienced in throwing all responsibility on others.
6. Let him read any printed matter he can get his hands on. Be careful that the silverware and drinking glasses are sterilized, but let his mind feast on garbage.
7. Quarrel frequently in the presence of your children. In this way they will not be too shocked when the home is broken up later.
8. Give a child all the spending money he wants. Never let him earn his own. Why should he have things as tough as you had them?
9. Satisfy his every craving for food, drink, and comfort. See that every sensual desire is gratified. Denial may lead to harmful frustration.
10. Take his part against neighbors, teachers, policemen. They are all prejudiced against your child.
11. When he gets into real trouble, apologize for yourself by saying, "I never could do anything with him."
12. Prepare for a life of grief. You will be likely to have it.

Issued by the Police Department of Houston, Texas.
Reprinted in NSSA Link, Nov. 1963.

GOD GIVES US CHILDREN. . .

1. To enjoy immediately—not to be somehow endured until they grow up.
2. To contribute to eternal values—to become soul winners, to bring spiritual blessings in the lives of others.
3. To bring comfort in old age—fellowship, grandchildren, security.
4. To contribute positive values to the world—"givers—not takers," good citizens, builders of society, "salt."
5. To bring a sense of personal completeness and fulfillment—self-extension, sense of posterity, a mark on the sands of time.
6. To broaden and develop and enrich the home—another facet and quality to the home.

CHILDREN LEARN WHAT THEY LIVE

If a child lives with criticism, he learns to condemn.
If a child lives with hostility, he learns to fight.
If a child lives with ridicule, he learns to be shy.
If a child lives with shame, he learns to feel guilty.
If a child lives with tolerance, he learns to be patient.
If a child lives with encouragement, he learns confidence.
If a child lives with praise, he learns to appreciate.
If a child lives with fairness, he learns justice.
If a child lives with security, he learns to have faith.
If a child lives with approval, he learns to like himself.
If a child lives with acceptance and friendship, He learns to find
    love in the world.

—Source unknown.

DISCIPLINE OF LITTLE ONES

1. Make a distinct difference between social error and moral error. Don't treat them in the same way when you discipline. If a child runs in the house in a hurry and slams the door, that may annoy you but it is not the same kind of wrong as lying or sassing or disobeying parents.

2. Don't try to discipline children by yelling. "Talk softly but carry a big stick" may make good sense politically; it makes even better sense in the matter of discipline. The occasions when you really feel you must raise your voice should be so rare that the sound will convince your children that judgment is about to fall immediately. A child soor. learns

to turn off the sound of a mother who indulges in constant yelling and repeated threats.

3. When you are working on a particular problem area in a child's life, learn not to "see" every single thing the child does wrong. If you are teaching him not to talk back, or not to tell lies, then you may have to work with him repeatedly several times a day to get these problems fixed. On these days you may have to be careful NOT TO NOTICE that he is talking with his mouth full or that he has come to the table without washing his hands. A child can be made to feel he is hopeless if he is continually badgered and corrected about everything.

On the other hand, if you DO make a point of telling him to wash his hands and he does not do so, then of course you will have to follow through on that order. Any deliberate disobedience cannot be ignored, although an unintentional oversight should perhaps occasionally be ignored to give emphasis to a more important issue.

4. Touch them. Hug them. Tell them frequently that you love them. This is especially important in connection with discipline.

5. Teach them many Scriptures while they are young. Quote the Bible to them often. Make sure you apply the Word of God to the daily problems that come up in the home.

6. Keep mealtime a happy time. Don't use the dinner table for discipline or discussing problems.

7. Never let a little one go to bed without a prayer, a kiss and some sweet word.

8. Make your children lovable, enjoyable. Don't raise them to be spoiled and obnoxious. It is fine to say that all children are sweet and beautiful, but that isn't so. A child who is allowed to behave badly is not a joy to be around and is a bad testimony to the Christian home.

9. Do not threaten a child with a spanking unless you intend to carry it out immediately when the offence occurs. Your child will recognize your dishonesty and learn that he cannot trust your word.

10. When you spank a child, do it thoroughly so that there is no anger or resentment when it is over. If a child is still screaming and angry, the job is not finished. The child should be taught to say, "I'm sorry. I was wrong." The parent should remind the child that he is too valuable to be allowed to grow up wrong, then the parent should love and pray for the child before he is dismissed.

"Suffer the little children to come unto me, and forbid them not: for of such is the kingdom of God."— Mark 10:14.

RULES MRS. WESLEY SET UP FOR HER CHILDREN AT HOME

1. No eating between meals.
2. All children in bed by 8:00 p.m.
3. Take your medicine without complaining.
4. Subdue self-will in each child.
5. Work with God to save the soul of each child.
6. Teach child to pray as soon as he can speak.
7. Require all to be still during family worship.
8. Give children nothing they cry for.
9. Give them only what they ask for politely.
10. To prevent lying, punish no fault which is first confessed.
11. Don't allow a sinful act to go unpunished.
12. Preserve property rights, even in the smallest matters.
13. Command and reward good behavior.
14. Strictly observe all promises.
15. Require no daughter to work before she can read well.
16. Teach children to fear the rod.

CHILDREN

I took a piece of plastic clay
And I idly fashioned it one day.
And as my fingers pressed it still,
It moved and yielded to my will.
I came again when days were past;
The bit of clay was hard at last.
The form I gave it still it bore,
But I could change that form no more.

I took a piece of living clay,
And I touched it gently day by day;
And molded with my power and art,
A young child, soft and yielding heart.
And I came again when years were gone;
It was a man, a man I looked upon.
That early impress still he wore,
And I could change that form no more.

—Author Unknown.

"Verily I say unto you, Except ye be converted, and become as little children, ye shall not enter into the kingdom of heaven."—Matt. 18:3.

A RAINY-DAY PROJECT FOR CHILDREN

You will need: A small piece of plywood or very heavy cardboard (corrugated will do); seeds such as watermelon, various types of dried beans, popping corn, split peas, sunflower seeds, pumpkin seeds, wheat, rice, etc., and a bottle of glue or small dish of flour paste.

1. Draw a picture on plywood or heavy cardboard. (Avoid using very small, intricate designs.)

2. Fill in the design by gluing down various seeds. The seeds may be placed on the design individually or, if you are using small seeds, you can sprinkle many of them on at one time. You may use the seeds to cover the entire picture (like a mosaic), or you may paint or color the picture first and use the seeds to add texture. (Rice can be colored ahead of time by dipping into a solution of water and a few drops of food coloring.) If you do not have a large variety of seeds, you can use dry macaroni and broken pieces of spaghetti.

3. When the picture is dry, spray with hairspray. (If this is to be kept permanently, it should be varnished.)

"IS THIS THE SUM OF MOTHERHOOD?"

1965:

. . .the smell of bubble gum?

. . .a muddy footprint on the kitchen floor?

. . .the minutes, hour-long until a waited child comes in the door?

. . .a sudden fear. . .the feel of hot dry skin and fever in the night?

. . .to stop a childish fuss and then decipher who was wrong—or right?

. . .a thousand questions, such as "Where does wind begin?" and "Tell me how birds fly."

. . .Whose answers from the birth of time have puzzled wiser folk than I.

"And let us not be weary in well doing: for in due season we shall reap, if we faint not."—Gal. 6:9.

No, there is more. . .

1975:

. . .a quiet confidence shared when all the house is still.

. . .self-conscious hopes observed, and fuzzy dreams, and yet—a firm resolve to do God's will.

. . .to watch the choices made: "Is this the girl, the school, the work for me?" (Such weighty choices for so young a heart!)

. . .to wonder at the future, bright yet hard to see?

"That our sons may be as plants grown up in their youth; that our

daughters may be as corner stones, polished after the similitude of a palace:. . .Happy is that people, that is in such a case: yea, happy is that people whose God is the Lord."—Ps. 144:13, 15.

1985:

. . .These are the arrows I will send abroad. Each day these precious shafts who have been within my care will count somehow—for time and Heaven too.

. . .My deepest longings as a mother will be met if I have kept them polished, straight and true.

"Lo, children are an heritage of the Lord: and the fruit of the womb is his reward. As arrows are in the hand of a mighty man: so are children of the youth. Happy is the man that hath his quiver full of them: they shall not be ashamed, but they shall speak with the enemies in the gate."—Ps. 127:3-5.

—Jessie Sandberg.

TECHNIQUES FOR MAKING HOME IMPORTANT TO YOUR CHILDREN

By Don and Jessie Sandberg

1. Display certificates of honor, newspaper clippings of sports activities, family pictures, art work. Allow children to have their own bulletin boards.

2. Teach your children *HOW* to work and give them important regular jobs to do in the home.

3. Don't hesitate to discuss financial needs and other emergencies with your children.

4. Don't save all your "fixing up" for company. Set the table nicely and plan special treats and desserts.

5. Make family traditions important—Christmas, family vacations, birthdays, etc.

6. Let children have a few private places—the loft of the garage, an attic corner. Don't feel you have to "clean" a child's play area too often. Let them have a corner to handle their own way.

7. Keep materials and tools available so that children can pursue creative activities—boxes, paper, scotch tape, glue, scraps of wood and cloth.

8. Encourage family projects: music, model railroads, building castle or doll houses, games, baking cookies (example: children's "Sum-

mer Club—1970"; colonial dinner), picnics at the lake, weight-lifting, picking fruit (blueberry farm).

9. Make your children's friends welcome.

10. Pray with your children about every problem that comes up. Help them get used to expecting God's help.

11. Be affectionate openly. Don't be afraid to say, "I love you," or, "I'm glad we have you." (Example: father who would never kiss or hug her.)

12. Give your children the security of seeing that their father and mother still love and enjoy each other. They need this assurance.

13. Make family devotions important. Even a small child should get used to hearing the Word of God read and hearing his parents pray.

14. Don't leave any problem in the family unresolved so that resentment and bitterness develop. Talk it out, pray it out, and love it out.

15. Enjoy your own uniqueness as a family. You don't have to set your lifestyle by what other people do, and you don't have to judge the success of your home by the *things* in it.

16. Enjoy your children. Laugh and play with them. Let them teach you some things. Listen to their stories, their dreams, their problems. Look at them; appreciate their special qualities and individual characteristics.

HOW TO BUILD SELF-CONFIDENCE IN YOUR CHILDREN
By Mrs. Douglas Cravens

1. Be very sensitive to the feelings of your child. Never ridicule him. Do not in any way crush his spirit. You do, however, have to break his will. Do not even tease him about things that embarrass him. Be careful not to embarrass him in public. Punishment should be done in private.

2. Compliment and praise your child on inner qualities such as patience, unselfishness, diligence, and truthfulness, rather than on outward beauty (as the world sees beauty), a beauty that the child had nothing to do with.

3. Respect your child. Listen to his ideas. Follow through on many of them.

4. Slow down your pace and take time for each child. He needs to

know that he is so important to you that you want time with him separately and that you enjoy being with him. Make him feel secure.

5. Love him unconditionally. Accept him as he is. Never indicate to him in any way that you or God would stop loving him when he is "bad." Teach him that God loves him unconditionally.

7. Show him early that God made him different from everybody else. He did this for a special purpose: to glorify God. God the Creator does not make anyone ugly. "God does not make copies, only originals."

8. Help your child to see his strengths and weaknesses. Help him capitalize on the strengths and get help on his weak points (if they are important).

9. Get him involved in projects that will teach him to reach out (extend himself) to meet the needs of others.

10. Teach him to do some things well so that he can develop confidence in his abilities.

11. Lead your child to accept Christ as his Saviour as soon as he really understands. Teach him from the Word and by example that God should be *first* in his life. Show him how to develop a close relationship with God and how to grow in the Lord.

12. Help him grow emotionally, socially, mentally, and physically.

13. Do not allow brothers and sisters (or others in your home) to cut each other down.

14. Explain that the world's system of values is not Christian. Tell him that we get our values from the Word, which teaches that we are to become Christlike. Show him the way to do this. Make it a family project. Beauty, intellect, and money are worshiped by the world. God hates this as a value of a person's worth.

15. Teach your child to handle guilt (I John 1:9).

16. Encourage him to make friends. Bring friends into your home and observe him and his friends. You may be able to see what he needs in the matter of self-esteem.

17. Warn your preteens that they will naturally have some feelings of inadequacy during their teens, but that it does not mean they are unworthy.

18. Give your preteen a good sense of self-awareness by helping him to know his goals, his good points, his weak points, his ambitions. Show him what God thinks about him and his life.

19. Teach the Christian attitude toward sex and the opposite sex. There is an important relationship between low self-esteem and immorality.

20. Someone must believe in your child if he is to grow up happy and able to cope. Will you be that someone?

21. To see Mother and Dad showing love to each other is a tremendous security builder in your child and teaches him to love.

22. Have you ever thought how unfair it is to children and adults for you to make these comments? "You pinhead. Can't you get anything straight?" "Oh, what a beautiful child!" "Honey, you are the prettiest thing I ever saw!" "Oh, hello, Johnny. Are you doing better in school?" "Where did you get those big ears?" "Aren't you gaining weight again?" "What are you doing for those pimples?" "Haven't you started dating yet?" "What is the matter with you?" Never say, "How stupid!" "You are so dumb!" "Why can't you be like Joe?" "You just look a mess." "When will you ever grow up?" "You are a bad girl." "Why isn't a nice girl like you married?"

WOULD THESE BE BETTER? "Isn't she a friendly child?" "You surely did a good job when you made that dress." "Thank you for your excellent solo. I know you worked hard on that." "Mary, you were so unselfish when you did that." "I appreciate your being honest in this matter. I know that took courage."

HOW TO DEVELOP GREATNESS IN YOUR CHILDREN
By Mrs. Don Sandberg

1. Surround your children with good books and good music. Encourage a love for reading.

2. Help your children to learn to recognize the consequences of sin.

3. Make your home a happy place to be.

4. Encourage Scripture memorization at an early age. Establish a family altar.

5. Teach your children to enjoy work.

6. Encourage your children to learn something that will help them develop confidence in themselves. Provide lessons and give support and encouragement.

7. Be generous with praise. Take time to listen to your children. Discuss family needs and other problems freely with your children.

Allow your children to express their feelings and to question.

8. Make a big thing of family celebrations and traditions. Give your children links to their past. Help them develop family pride.

9. Teach independence and self-reliance. Help your children to learn to make decisions.

10. Welcome your children's friends into the home. Make your house a gathering place for friends and neighbors.

11. Help your children learn how to handle disappointment.

12. Let your marriage be a model that your children will be happy to copy. Show that you like each other as well as love each other.

13. Do all you can do to help your child build happy memories.

14. Show your child that privilege brings with it responsibility.

15. Teach your children to have respect for themselves and for other people. Help them to see that respect is a prerequisite for love; that respect for other people is an important aspect of leadership.

16. Win your children to the Lord at an early age and help them day by day to learn to have a strong reliance upon the Word of God and to learn that prayer is the answer to all life's problems.

BIRTHSTONES, FLOWERS AND
WEDDING ANNIVERSARIES

Month	Stone	Flower
January	GARNET for constancy	CARNATION for friendship
February	AMETHYST for sincerity	VIOLET for modesty
March	BLOODSTONE for courage	JONQUIL for affection
April	DIAMOND for innocence	SWEET PEA for love
May	EMERALD for happiness	LILY OF THE VALLEY for purity
June	PEARL for purity	ROSE for devotion
July	RUBY for nobility	LARKSPUR for haughtiness
August	SARDONYX for felicity	GLADIOLUS for preparedness
September	SAPPHIRE for wisdom	ASTER for memories
October	OPAL for hope	CALENDULA for constancy
November	TOPAZ for fidelity	CHRYSANTHEMUM for loveliness
December	TURQUOISE for success	NARCISSUS for precious moments

WEDDING ANNIVERSARIES

First	paper	13th	lace
2nd	cotton	14th	ivory
3rd	leather	15th	crystal
4th	fruit and flowers	20th	china
5th	wood	25th	silver
6th	sugar and candy	30th	pearl
7th	woolen or pottery	35th	coral
8th	bronze or pottery	40th	ruby
9th	pottery or willow	45th	sapphire
10th	tin	50th	golden
11th	steel	55th	emerald
12th	silk and linen	60th and 75th	diamond

THANKSGIVING PLACE CARD

Thanksgiving Day is a time for families, no matter how scattered, to come together. Brothers and sisters, aunts, uncles, and cousins all enjoy the holiday and spend the day catching up on family news, singing together and thanking God for His blessings throughout the year. Here is an idea for a Thanksgiving place card you can make to decorate the holiday table.

Materials needed:

one apple per person
box of toothpicks (colored or plain)
stiff cardboard
colored pencils or water colors

Directions:

Cut out a shape of a turkey's head and neck from the cardboard, using pattern below. Slit the apple slightly, and place the turkey head approximately in the center. Stick toothpicks in the apple to make a tail, flaring them slightly.

Using the colored pencils, write the person's name on a small piece of cardboard and fold back the edges to slip into the front of the apple. Place in front of each place setting.

Optional: The toothpicks may be painted to add more color. The turkey head may be colored with pencils or water colors.

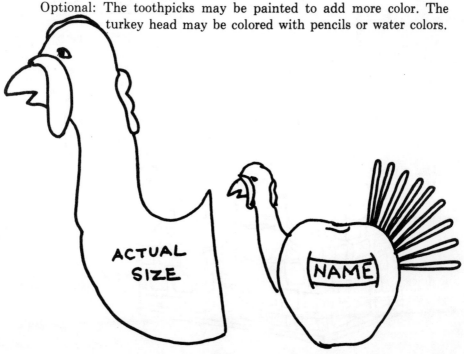

ACTUAL SIZE

NAME

HOW TO MAKE A CANDY HOUSE

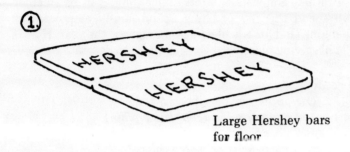

① Large Hershey bars
for floor

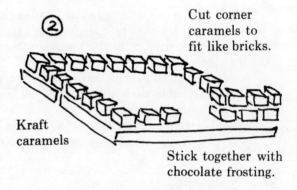

② Cut corner
caramels to
fit like bricks.

Kraft
caramels

Stick together with
chocolate frosting.

You may need an ice cream stick or
candy canes to carry weight of roof.

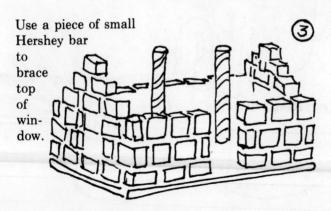

Use a piece of small
Hershey bar
to
brace
top
of
win-
dow.

③

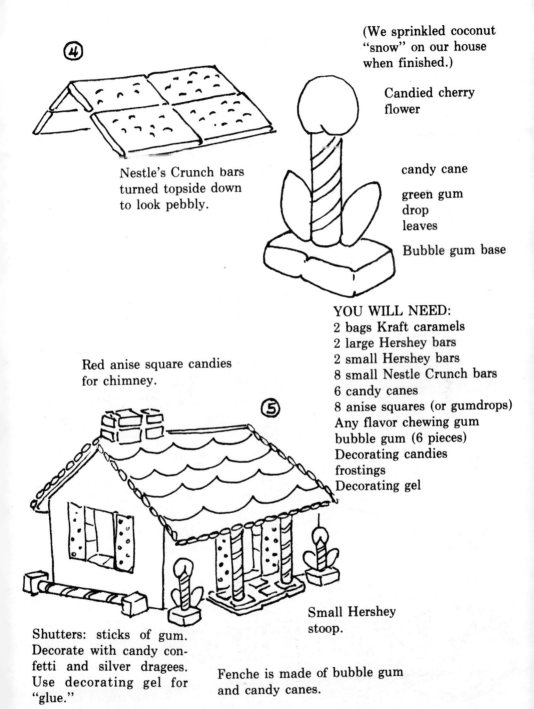

④

(We sprinkled coconut "snow" on our house when finished.)

Candied cherry flower

Nestle's Crunch bars turned topside down to look pebbly.

candy cane

green gum drop leaves

Bubble gum base

YOU WILL NEED:
2 bags Kraft caramels
2 large Hershey bars
2 small Hershey bars
8 small Nestle Crunch bars
6 candy canes
8 anise squares (or gumdrops)
Any flavor chewing gum
bubble gum (6 pieces)
Decorating candies
frostings
Decorating gel

Red anise square candies for chimney.

⑤

Small Hershey stoop.

Shutters: sticks of gum. Decorate with candy confetti and silver dragees. Use decorating gel for "glue."

Fenche is made of bubble gum and candy canes.

STAINED GLASS ORNAMENTS

You will need:
  white glue
  gift-wrap cord
  plastic wrap
  food coloring
  toothpicks
  glitter

1. Anchor a piece of plastic wrap to a piece of cardboard with tape.

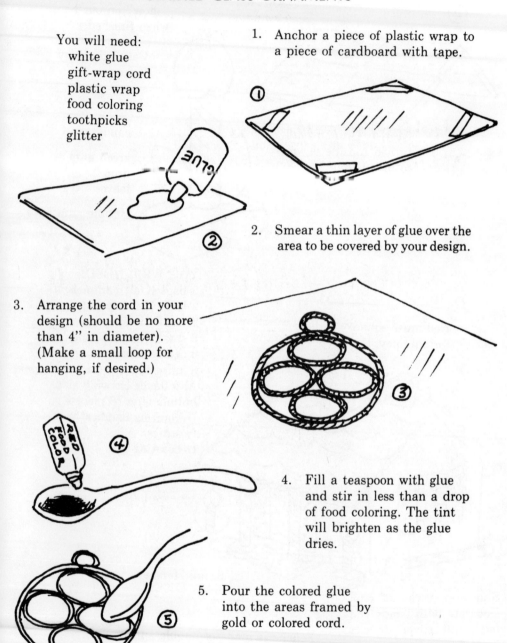

2. Smear a thin layer of glue over the area to be covered by your design.

3. Arrange the cord in your design (should be no more than 4" in diameter). (Make a small loop for hanging, if desired.)

4. Fill a teaspoon with glue and stir in less than a drop of food coloring. The tint will brighten as the glue dries.

5. Pour the colored glue into the areas framed by gold or colored cord.

6. Add glitter or sequins.

7. Let the ornament dry for several days (Don't be impatient!). When the glue is completely dry, the ornament will be transparent. Peel off the plastic wrap. If you did not make a small loop for hanging, make a hole near the tip and tie on a small ribbon for hanging. .

* * * *

"Inflexibility and insensitivity are related."

"When you are 'bumped' what splashes out? Whatever is on the inside will splash out when hit."

"We have grace notes in music—not essential but thrown in to make the score more beautiful—that's what kindness does."

"Love is the Christian's badge. Do you wear it?"
—Michael Guido

"God may humble you, but He will not humiliate you."
—Jack Hyles

"Jealousy is the tribute that mediocrity pays to greatness."
—Jack Hyles

"Champions are not born; they're made."
—Jerry Falwell

"You are what you produce."
—Dr. Bob Jones, Sr.

An Assortment

...of friends and relatives

FAMILY

I am nobody
But I belong to a special
    group of people called "Family."
My family has struggled
    through the years of my learning,
      falling down
          piano lessons
              and falling down again.
    To make me what I am today.
    My family molded me,
      formed my personality.
I could survive shipwreck
    and famine
But I'm lost without a family.
I may be a nobody in the world
But at home I'm special
    because I'm part of a family.
I have someone to come home to.
    I belong.
I am loved by a real, live family.

—Carol Sandberg, 1974.

Kind friend, I wish for you
    a package of courage
    a bag of good humor
    A mountain of wisdom
    A sea of smiles
    Quick eyes to see much
    Soft words to turn away wrath
    An antidote against the virus of self-love
    Blocks of steadfastness which bend not
    Sealed vaults to bury faults of friends.
    An unafraid heart to tell how Christ can save
    A tongue wherein the law of kindness ever dwells—
    Peace.

—Ruby Wagner.

FRIENDSHIP

Oh, the comfort, the inexpressible comfort
Of feeling safe with a person. . . . Having neither
To weigh thoughts nor measure words,
But pouring them all right out,
Chaff and grain together, certain that
Faithful hand will take and sift them—
Keep what is worth keeping and with a breath of
Kindness, blow the rest away.

—Author unknown.

"Love is blind; friendship tries not to notice."
—Otto Von Bismarck.

BACK ROOM

I have opened the door of my heart
To invite some into the parlor there
*   For conversation and exchange of wit*
*   And polite laughter while we primly sit.*

I have opened my parlor door
To others who may come inside
*   And find my tears still on my face*
*   And sobs in my voice, if that be the case.*

But you I take to my heart's back room,
Untidy with confusion and fear;
*   And you willingly help to make it bright*
*   As you straighten and clean and let in the light.*

—Jewel Martin.

FATHERS ARE NICE

A father is nice when you're little because when he comes home from work you can take out his leftover lunch and have a picnic in the closet.

A father is good at playing hide-and-seek and even though he can't seem to find good hiding places where you don't find him, he is still fun to play with.

A father is fun when you can ride on his shoulders and look at the world from a different view.

And a father is nice when he's gardening and you're helping and he saves a worm for you.

When Mom is having a woman's meeting at the house and you don't want to listen to a bunch of ladies talking, fathers are good at making popcorn and keeping you entertained.

A father is nice when you're big because he understands how important it is to have a room of your own when you're the only girl in the family. And a father is nice too when you're the only girl because he likes you to have pretty coats and dresses.

Fathers provide you with food and clothing and love. Fathers are a picture of courage and trust. Fathers tell you about the Lord and why they love Him and why they want you to love Him.

Fathers are the most understanding people in the world. You can tell them anything you want and they're always ready to help.

Fathers are wonderful for lots of things, but best of all, for loving.

—Carol Sandberg (at 13 years of age).

DR. BOB SHULER TELLS ABOUT HIS FATHER

Among my earliest vivid recollections was an early morning scene in the little mountain house where we lived. My father and mother were earnestly talking; he was telling her that he felt he was called to preach. We had practically nothing to leave, but I recall that a great shock of surprise overwhelmed me as I realized that my father proposed to move out bag and baggage (though we had neither) and become a circuit rider . . . .

And strange as it may seem. . .I entered into a solemn covenant with my own childish soul to help Mother and the good Lord make a preacher of my father.

Through the winter and spring, I took him to Elk Creek Academy (he had not so much as finished the second reader in the schools). I took him down every Monday morning and went after him with "Old Bet" and "Old Bird" every Friday afternoon. I did the chores with a new enthusiasm.

The following summer we harnessed "Old Bet" and "Old Bird" to the covered wagon and went across Iron Mountain to Emory and Henry College at Emory, Virginia. The best house we could get was a little shack under the railroad bank. . .I recall that Dr. Atkins. . .was the president of Emory and Henry. Just before the school term opened he met my father on the railroad right-of-way. I was standing by. Here's about what he said:

"Brother Shuler, I admire your enthusiasm and daring very much, but you have no educational background and have made no preparation to enter this college. You can't make the courses. You have a wife and five children and, I understand, no money. Somebody should have advised you. There is a large place for local preachers in the mountain community where you came up. You simply started too late and with too many encumbrances to think of making an itinerant preacher."

I think he convinced my father. But he didn't count on mother. When she got through with that incident, all the devils in perdition couldn't have stopped that pair. That same year, my father led a Senior class in English literature and an amazed college president called this mountaineer into his office and apologized for some very faulty advice he had given.

Years after that, at the West Texas Annual Conference at which Bishop Atkins was presiding, I heard him tell that story and say, "From that hour I have never tried to tell a man, whom God had called to preach, what he could do and what he could not do."

—From *Bob Shuler Met These on the Trail.*

WHAT A GRANDMOTHER IS
(By a child)

A grandmother is a lady who has no children of her own. She likes other people's little girls. A grandfather is a man grandmother. He goes for walks with the boys and they talk about fishing and tractors and like that.

Grandmothers don't have to do anything but be there. They're old, so they shouldn't play hard or run. It is enough if they drive us to the market where the Pretend-Horse is, and have lots of dimes ready. Or if they take us for walks, they should slow down passing things, like pretty leaves or caterpillars. They should never say, "Hurry up."

Usually they are fat, but not too fat to tie your shoes. They wear glasses and funny underwear. They can take their teeth and gums off. . . .

They don't have to be smart, only answer questions like "Why dogs hate cats," and "How come God isn't married?"

They don't talk baby talk like visitors do, because it is hard to understand. When they read to us, they don't skip words or mind if it is the same story again.

Everybody should try to have one, especially if you don't have television, because grandmas are the only grownups who have got time!"

—from THE MIAMI HERALD.

A More Creative You!

HOW TO BE A CREATIVE WIFE

1. Plan things to do together and with the family that you know your husband would enjoy but won't go to the trouble to plan for himself.

2. If you know he hates to buy gifts, tell him three things you like (size, color, brand specified) and tell him where they can be bought. If he does dare to launch out and buy something on his own, be enthusiastic and thankful about his gift. If the size is wrong and can be exchanged without any "to-do," simply do so without any comment. If you are not happy with the color, you may need to say, "You know, Honey, I've sort of been yearning for a blue sweater to go with that blue plaid skirt I have. I just love the style of the sweater you bought. What do you think of my exchanging it for one of a slightly different shade?" The point is to be careful not to hurt his pride or to make a big deal of insisting on satisfying your own taste always, to the exclusion of his. (Did you know that most husbands who buy clothes for their wives pick out more expensive, better garments than a wife would choose for herself?)

3. Don't always react the predictable way in a given situation. Watch out for comments like, "I *knew* you would say that!" When your husband does something that doesn't turn out right, you may need to learn to say, "I'm sorry that didn't turn out like you hoped it would, Honey. Would it help to talk about it? I'm sure there's a way to work out the problem."

4. Don't use every conversation as an occasion to hammer home some point you've been trying to prove.

5. Listen for clues your husband may be dropping about things he would like to see changed. If he teases you about the way your hair looks at the breakfast table, he may be gently telling you that he would like to see you pay more attention to the way you look. Don't just make excuses for the particular problems he points out; make a mental note that you will keep that problem from coming up again.

6. Interpret correctly the messages he sends you. Ideally, all married couples should verbally express their love for each other. It is also important for everyone to learn to say, "I'm sorry," "I made a mistake," "I feel grouchy," etc. But this has always been easier for women than for men, and there may be times when a wife must read a message of love in an act even when it is not spoken in words.

"We are apt to say that submission would never be a problem if God would give His orders personally, but He has chosen to use the faulty telephone system of other human beings who are in authority over us, and He expects us to obey."

—J.R.S.

One young husband, coming from a childhood spent in an orphanage, had a very difficult time in the early years of marriage expressing the way he felt about his wife. Instead, he would buy her clothes or flowers or candy, and although he sometimes seemed rather casual about such gifts, his wife learned to understand that he was deliberately trying to express something very deep and very precious.

7. While there should never be any question about the position of the husband's authority in the home, there should be occasions when you relieve him of the responsibility of making decisions that you know will not displease him. Sometimes, when my husband would come home late in the evening after some very wearing responsibility, I would ask, "What can I fix you to eat?" I soon learned that he was really too tired to want to plan about food. Many husbands would really rather have a wife "take over" at such a time—to lay out his robe and pajamas, to begin running a hot bath and to have something all ready for him to eat. He might even want all telephone calls intercepted and the children quietly taken care of without his having to handle family matters that would usually be his responsibility. You will know how your husband feels about these things if you take time to notice his reactions under stress.

8. Don't make your husband feel guilty about any sacrifices you must make in helping your husband: working while he is in school, doing without something so he can start his own business, etc. Make it easy for your husband to grow. (Does he want to go back to school? Does he feel God is calling him into some ministry? Encourage him and back him, even if it means some sacrifice for you. God will make it turn out right!)

9. Make it your responsibility to add lightness and life in the home. Your husband didn't marry you just so he would have someone to wash his clothes and bear his children. He needs you to add color, softness, beauty and joy to his life.

10. Gently and lovingly help your husband to reach his best potential—in the way he looks and dresses, the way he speaks, in his dealings with others. If you resort to nagging, you will do more harm than good.

11. Be single-minded in your attention to his needs. Nothing—absolutely nothing—in the world should come before your being the kind of wife God intended you to be—not your children, your church work or your personal ambitions. Keep your bedroom a quiet, clean and private place—a haven for you two alone. (This is *not* the place to leave laundry waiting to be folded, or yesterday's newspapers lying around.)

No schedule will work out perfectly, but as far as you are able, plan your late evenings so there will be time for a relaxing bath, a hot cup of tea (or a Coke, if you prefer) together and a few minutes to talk before you go to bed. Many a husband is frustrated by a well-meaning wife who works frantically until bedtime and then falls into bed exhausted and totally unresponsive to her husband's needs.

12. View your marriage as a gift to be cherished and nurtured. HANDLE WITH CARE—polish it gently; protect it from the ravages of wear; enjoy it with gratitude to the God who designed the institution as a beautiful symbol of the relationship between the dear Lord Jesus and His beloved church.

Never forget that you married your husband for what he was—not for what you hoped he would be. Don't consider yourself responsible for "hammering" him into what you think you want in a husband. You will make marks that can never be erased. Love him; enjoy him; find pleasure in his own endearing traits; accept him for what he is. You will find that you have made an investment that will count for eternity.

CREATIVITY IN THE HOME

1. Start looking, smelling, seeing. Learn to enjoy the things you have around you all the time that you take for granted.
2. Start a file—recipes, poems, stories for the children, etc.
3. Learn to sew.
4. Try a new hairdo once in a while.
5. Start keeping a journal.
6. Try writing a poem.
7. Make your own birthday cards.
8. Make your own Christmas gifts.
9. Try some new exercises; a new diet. If you don't like the way you look, CHANGE!
10. Provide materials and tools for children's projects. Be generous with Scotch tape, paper, paste.
11. Give your children a corner where they can work on projects for an extended time.
12. Let your children cook—encourage learning special recipes. Teach them the responsibility for cleaning up their own mess.
13. Make a big thing of birthdays and family traditions.
14. Learn when and how to break routine. When children get restless, try a backyard or a "fireplace" picnic. Why not serve ice cream or hot dogs for breakfast just for the fun of it.
15. Keep a box of old clothes and costumes for play and pretending.

16. Invest in books, records, music, inexpensive pictures.
17. Find a way to provide special lessons in art, music, etc. (If you can't afford to pay, exchange services—laundry, baking, babysitting, etc.).
18. Learn to use fabric remnants, Contact plastic, and paint, to make an old house fresh and pretty.
19. Learn to grow cheap plants: avacado, potato, orange seeds.
20. Learn to refinish furniture, upholster simple pieces, mat pictures, make bookcases, improvise lighting. Become an expert at some do-it-yourself technique. You can always trade services with other mothers if you have a special skill of your own.
21. Experiment with cake decorating.
22. Learn to make yeast bread.
23. Always set a pretty table even when only the family is home—always a place mat and paper napkin and often a nice tablecloth.
24. Learn to make your own candles (using paper cups, tin cans and other available molds) and burn them frequently. Candles always look like a celebration!
25. Look for weeds and wild flowers that will fill a pretty pot in summer; learn how to dry flowers for pretty winter bouquets.

Your home is a showplace for your own personality. It is the background for your children's dreams, the substance of their happiest memories. It is the haven to which your husband's heart must long to fly when the pressures of the world outside get too heavy. Do not neglect to fill it with beauty, with joyful surprises and happy communication. Above all, let your home reflect the sweetness of God's presence day by day. Let your work be done with commitment and contentment and your rest be accompanied with laughter and with praise.

—Jessie Sandberg.

PRINCIPLES OF CREATIVITY

1. Creativity is a gift of God and carries with it the responsibility for development and use.
2. Awareness is a major element of creativity. It is also essential to the Christian who wants to be a good marriage partner, a good parent and an effective soul winner.
3. Creativity is an attribute not related to intellectual genius. It cannot be measured by standard I.Q. tests.
4. Creative people are not easily bored.
5. Creative people do not need other people's attention to be happy.

6. Creative people learn to make the most of the present; they do not wait for better opportunities, for more leisure time.

7. Creative people learn how to use "wasted" time—minutes spent waiting in lines, sitting in doctors' offices, etc.

8. Creative people are more fun to be around.

9. Creative people always have a project they are working on. They keep notes of ideas they hope to work out in the future.

10. Creative people learn to work around the obstacle of limited money.

11. Creative people are not frustrated with experiments that fail. They learn what they can and try again.

12. Creative people tend to promote creativity in others.

13. Creative children are not apt to fall into temptations related to idleness.

14. Creative people tend to be fulfilled, satisfied individuals.

15. Creative people look at changes in life and new experiences as opportunities to learn and grow.

16. Creative people are curious people. They are not afraid to ask questions.

17. Creative people are readers. They want to know how other people react to life and solve problems.

CULTIVATE THE ART OF THINKING. . .by Reading

Nothing is as easy as thinking. And nothing is as difficult as thinking well.

Thinking well may be profitable, but if it is, it is always painful. There is a price tag to thinking well.

I saw this sign in a businessman's office some time ago which jarred me: "You are not what you think you are. What you think, you are." I was reminded of Proverbs 23:7, "For as he thinketh in his heart, so is he . . . ."

Thinking is always dangerous unless it is under the direction of the Spirit of God. Then it is eminently profitable. Philippians 4:8 says, "Finally, brethren, whatever is true, whatever is honorable, whatever is just, whatever is pure, whatever is lovely, whatever is gracious, if there is any excellence, if there is anything worthy of praise, think about these things."

Thinking has nothing to do with age, but it has everything to do with attitude. There is an epitaph that says, "Died—age 28. Buried—age 64." Unfortunately, that is the story of too many lives.

I have a lady friend who is 86 years old. Some time ago both of us were at a social gathering. When she spotted me, the first thing she said was, "Well, what are the best five books you've read in the last months?"

After a little conversation, she said, "Look, let's not bore one another with each other. Let's get into a discussion. And if we can't find anything to discuss, let's get into an argument." There she is—86 years old and still thinking strong!

Her first question was about reading. And in my judgment, one of the most crucial means of stretching your mind is through the process of reading.

Readers are leaders. And leaders are readers.

The mind is like a muscle. It develops with use. You won't wear it out. No one ever dies with a brain that has been totally used. That will never happen. Though you do need to constantly stretch your mind, be careful what you feed it, because what you feed it will largely determine what you are.

Perhaps you don't have a formal education. You can get the most profound education that it is possible to get. . .simply by reading. By reading you can pick the greatest minds of all the centuries.

Here are some tips on how to cultivate the art of thinking by reading:

Read widely and wisely.

Everything in print is not worth reading, even in the Christian bookstores. Read as widely as possible, because this is the way to stretch your mind.

I read books that I don't agree with, for example. If an author does not stretch my thinking, he doesn't really help me much.

We tend to read books that confirm our prejudices because we are such insecure people. That's why most of us are not thinking. We are just rearranging our prejudices.

Most of us do too much post-hole thinking. That is, we dig down too deeply in one direction instead of moving over and digging another hole, getting another tangent of thought, another perspective. What I do, for example, when I'm studying the Scriptures is to dig another hole from another viewpoint. I imagine myself as a doctor when reading a particular passage in Luke; then I get the perspective of a medical man.

How to choose good books.

First, I always pick books primarily on the basis of the author. A significant author generally produces a significant book.

Second, I look for a book which has been on the market a sufficient period of time to prove its value. If a book has been around for awhile (and not just because it happens to be a book on sex or some sensational subject), then it tends to have quality. My primary sources are *Time, Atlantic Monthly, Harper's Magazine,* and the *Saturday Review.*

An example of a book that has survived the fads of the moment is Herman Harrell Horne's *Teaching Techniques of Jesus.* It goes back into the early 1900's. It is still in print and it ought to be. It is a classic. For Christian leaders it is "must" reading, because it deals with the whole process of how Jesus trained His disciples.

Third, I read books which are out of my particular realm, books out of my field. Right now I'm reading a book on architecture that is absolutely fascinating. I just finished one on ornithology, the study of birds. This is the kind of thing that gives you all sorts of enriching material. It can also make you a more interesting person.

Learn to read faster.

I read three books every week for a minimum and 35 journals every month. The only way you can do this is by learning to read better and faster.

If you don't read better and faster, then you're just going to have to settle for limited objectives. Norman Lewis' paperback, *How to Read Better and Faster,* will help your reading habits.

Learning to read faster is simply a process of discipline, nothing more or less. If you read faster, you will not only read more but you will retain more. Many people think that if they slow down, they will retain more. Nothing could be further from the truth. The truth is that if you speed up your reading, you will retain more.

If it takes you 20 minutes to read a book of the New Testament and you retain "x" amount, by learning to read better and faster, you can read the same book in 15 minutes and retain twice as much. That means that for the same amount of time you can get four times as much out of your reading.

Become a "snatch" reader.

I have reading material all over the house. When I have ten minutes here or there, I pull down the book and read. I do lots of reading at airports and on airplanes.

Try "in-depth" reading.

Some men develop the practice of reading quite a number of books (maybe 20 or 30) on the same subject for a period of time. This is effective. It gives you depth and breadth in a specific field that you don't get with the more scattered, wider type of reading.

My goal is to spend one hour daily reading and studying the Word. I spend one month per book and cover in depth twelve books of the Bible per year. I've been through the Bible like this about seven times in my life. I set this goal early in my ministry, for I wanted to be a minister of the Word of God.

Some books are to be reread.

You may reread some books, but they are rare ones. Sometimes you simply can't get it all in one reading. And, furthermore, you may not get all of it at your level of maturity. If you read the same book ten years from now, you get an altogether different perspective.

One book I've reread is John Milton Gregory's *The Seven Laws of Teaching.* It was written in the last century.

If men in the teaching field were to read this book annually, they'd never teach the same way again. I've been teaching in seminary for 21 years and have read the book every single year.

As Sir Francis Bacon said, "Some books are to be tasted, others to be swallowed, and some few to be chewed and digested." Start reading more to cultivate the art of thinking.

(This article is reprinted by permission from the April, 1972, issue of the *The Navigators Log.* It was written by Dr. Howard Hendricks, Chairman of the Christian Education Center, Dallas Theological Seminary. —Copied from *The Prairie Overcomer.*)

HOW TO MAKE POMANDER BALLS

Select a firm, medium-size orange and stud the entire surface with whole cloves (about ½ inch apart.) The cloves will preserve the orange as it dries into a fragrant sachet which will last for years.

Allow the orange to dry for two weeks (it will shrink in size) and then wrap in colorful net fabric and tie at the top with a ribbon.

These may be kept in dresser drawers or hung in closets to keep clothes sweet-smelling; they may be hung over a kitchen window or they may be used on the Christmas tree year after year.

This is a simple and inexpensive gift for a child to make.

Giving God His Proper Place

HOW GOD USES TROUBLE IN YOUR LIFE FOR GOOD

1. **Trouble builds your faith:**

   You do not know what God can do for you 'til you are totally dependent on Him.

   "For therein is the righteousness of God revealed from faith to faith; as it is written, The just shall live by faith."—Rom. 1:17.

   "For we walk by faith and not by sight."—II Cor. 5:7,

2. **Trouble develops patience.**

   "In patience possess your souls."

   "Count it all joy. . .Knowing this, that the trying of your faith worketh patience. But let patience have her perfect work, that ye may be perfect and entire, wanting nothing."—James 1:3,4.

3. **Trouble builds compassion for others.**

   "As a sponge absorbs moisture, so compassion absorbs the trouble of those it touches."

   "Finally, be ye all of one mind, having compassion one of another."—I Pet. 3:8.

   "Bear ye one another's burdens, and so fulfill the law of Christ."—Gal. 6:2.

4. **Trouble develops humility.**

   "Humble yourselves in the sight of the Lord and he shall build you up."—James 4:10.

   "Be clothed with humility."—I Pet. 5:5.

5. **Trouble teaches forgiveness.**

   "And be ye kind one to another, tenderhearted, forgiving one another, even as God for Christ's sake hath forgiven you."—Eph. 4:32.

   "Forgive us our debts as we forgive our debtors."—Matt. 6:8.

6. **Trouble directs our eyes toward Heaven.**

   "And to you who are troubled rest with us, when the Lord Jesus shall be revealed from heaven with his mighty angels, In flaming fire taking vengeance on them that know not God, and that obey not the gospel of our Lord Jesus Christ."—II Thess. 1:7,8.

7. **Trouble makes the Word of God sweet.**

   "Great peace have they which love thy law and nothing shall offend them."—Ps. 119:165.

   —Jessie Sandberg.

FAMILY DEVOTIONS AND SPIRITUAL GROWTH: HOW A WOMAN CAN HELP

1. Establish the fact in your own mind that your husband is the head of the home spiritually. Gently and persistently encourage him to take this responsibility.

2. Get used to saying to your husband, "Honey, would you pray with me about this particular problem?"

3. Share with your husband and children particular things that the Lord has taught you today: "I found the most exciting thing in my Bible reading today!"

4. Be ready to give spiritual encouragement during difficult times. Sometimes put a note in your husband's pocket or lunch that will be a special help for the day: "I love you. I noticed you were so tired last night. I'll be praying that the Lord will give you strength today." A particular Bible verse typed on a card might also be a help to your husband packed right along with the lunch.

5. Set up circumstances conducive to devotions: breakfast ready on time if family devotions are planned for the morning; lunches already prepared; snack dishes from the evening before already cleaned up. If devotions are planned for the evening, get dinner and dishes out of the way as soon as possible. Have children bathed and ready for bed. Both you and your family will be more prepared for family devotions if you have not been screaming and scolding just before you pull out the Bibles!

6. Keep your own attitude cheerful and happy regarding family devotions. If you approach it as a duty to be done, everybody else in the family will feel that way about it too.

7. Be careful not to criticize the way your husband conducts the family worship. His leadership is more important than your ideas of perfection.

8. Be patient and optimistic about establishing a good pattern of family devotions. If your husband is slow getting involved, be especially loving and supportive and encouraging. Make your family's spiritual growth a matter of prayerful concern.

9. Use the Scripture as an integral part of your family life. Apply its principles in child-rearing (and show your children specifically what the Bible says), in problem solving, and in relationships with other people. MAKE THE BOOK LIVE!

10. Make up your mind that your children will have the opportunity to see by personal example that God does answer prayer. Include the children in prayers for family needs. Encourage them to take their own problems to the Heavenly Father. (You will be thrilled to see the faith

your children develop in the promises of God!)

The key to successful family devotions and spiritual growth is faithfulness. If our children are to grow up in the nurture and admonition of the Lord, it will be because we have worked at it moment by moment, day by day and year by year. If our home is one in which Jesus Christ is given a place of honor, it will be because we have made that more important than anything else. But, oh, what wonderful results for our concern and labor! What special blessings God has for those who honor Him in this way!

"Whom shall he teach knowledge and whom shall he make to understand doctrine? them that are weaned from the milk, and drawn from the breasts. For precept must be upon precept, precept upon precept; line upon line, line upon line; here a little, and there a little."—Isa. 28:9,10.

"And these words, which I command thee this day, shall be in thy heart: And thou shalt teach them diligently unto thy children, and shalt talk of them when thou sittest in thine house, and when thou walkest by the way, and when thou liest down, and when thou risest up."—Deut. 6:6,7.

WORRY IS A SIN!

1. Worry is a lack of trust in the Lord. Worry denies that God can and will do what He promised to do.
2. Worry opens door for other sins. It encourages doubt and disbelief. It often leads to the wrong use of one's money and possessions.
3. Worry dulls the sweetness of the Word of God and discourages prayer.
4. Worry sours the disposition and shrinks the generous heart.
5. Worry stifles the song of praise and deadens the testimony of God's power in the life of the Christian.
6. Worry seals the lips of the soul winner and minimizes one's interest in missions.
7. Worry makes one's chosen work a chore to be somehow gotten through.
8. Worry brings physical exhaustion and innumerable little physical distresses. It kills joy and laughter and speeds up old age.
9. Worry robs a man of his sleep and makes leisure a bore. It dulls the pleasure of friendship, destroys dreams and goals and condemns one to a life of pettiness.

Dear friend, face it; worry is a sin! Until we are willing to admit how great a sin it is, we will not confess it and forsake it. How sad it is that so many Christians are leading lives of only partial usefulness and happiness because they have not learned to trust the Lord!

"Trust in the Lord, and do good; so shalt thou dwell in the land, and verily thou shalt be fed. Delight thyself also in the Lord; and he shall give thee the desires of thine heart."—Ps. 37:3,4.

DAILY LOSING YOUR LIFE

When I was a teenager, I once came across Matthew 10.09 in my daily devotional reading and I remember puzzling for a long time over its meaning. The passage reads: "He that findeth his life shall lose it; and he that loseth his life for my sake, shall find it." I had often heard missionaries quote the verse and I assumed that it referred entirely to one's physical life. Obviously, a martyr who gave his life for the cause of Christ would have some special reward in Heaven, and by the same token any Christian who refused to stand true to Christ in a time of great persecution was only wasting his life even though he saved it.

It was only after I became a grown woman that I began to understand that losing one's life for Christ's sake might have implications for Christians in the everyday routines of life—rearing children, keeping a home, working at a job, buying groceries, visiting with friends, teaching a Sunday school class—and so on.

Just recently, as I was searching my own heart about my willingness to "lose myself" for the cause of Christ, I made a list of those things which the Lord might require of me *today.*

To lose myself for the cause of Christ may mean:

1. To be willing to give up my privacy. Almost every kind of spiritual ministry requires involvement with people.

2. To be willing to accept a thousand little impositions on my schedule—taking time for telephone calls, little notes of encouragement, visits to the the unsaved, the ill, the bereaved—even when I have many other responsibilities.

3. To deny myself the satisfaction of being disgusted with people who are spoiled and backslidden and critical; to learn to love *anyway.*

4. To be willing to give cheerfully the things which other people require of me as a wife, a mother, a Sunday school teacher, a neighbor.

5. To squelch a natural tendency to nurse along my own hurts, and dwell on my own discomforts.

6. To refuse to allow myself to constantly analyze and hash over my

own weaknesses and imperfections and, instead, turning them over to the Lord.

7. To practice a life of faith even when I do not "feel" a deep faith. To make decisions and fulfill responsibilities not on the basis of what I can see, but on the basis of what God has promised.

8. To keep doing the job God has given, even in the face of opposition, ridicule, disappointment and seeming failure.

9. To seek the power of the Holy Spirit in my life even when I know that the fulness of the Holy Spirit may mean giving up some of the things which I have hitherto felt to be of top importance in my life.

10. To be willing to be misunderstood, slighted, maligned and taken for granted in doing the work God has given me to do.

Tell me, are *you* "losing yourself" today?

"THIS THING IS FROM ME"

My child, I have a message for you today; let me whisper it in your ear, that it may gild with glory any storm clouds which may arise, and smooth any of the rough places upon which you may have to tread.

It is short, only five words, but let them sink into your inmost soul, use them as a pillow upon which to rest your weary head:

THIS THING IS FROM ME

Have you ever thought of it, that all that concerns you, concerns Me, too? For 'he that toucheth you toucheth the apple of mine eye' (Zech. 2:9).

'You are very precious in my sight' (Isa. 43:4). Therefore, it is My special delight to educate you.

I would have you learn when temptations assail you, and the "enemy comes in like a flood," that this thing is from Me, that your weakness needs My might, and your safety lies in letting Me fight for you.

Are you in difficult circumstances, surrounded by people who do not understand you, who never consult your taste, who put you in the background? This thing is from Me. I am the God of circumstances. "Thou cam'st not to thy place by accident; it is the very place God meant for thee." Have you not asked to be made humble? See, then, I have placed you in the very school where this lesson is taught; your surroundings and companions are only working out My will.

Are you in money difficulties? Is it hard to make both ends meet? This thing is from Me, for I am your purse-bearer, and would have you draw from and depend upon Me. My supplies are limitless (Phil. 4:19). I would have you prove My promises. Let it not be said of you, "In this thing ye did not believe the Lord your God" (Deut. 1:32).

Are you passing through a night of sorrow? This thing is from Me. I am

"a man of sorrows, and acquainted with grief." I have let earthly com-
forters fail you, that by turning to Me you may obtain everlasting con-
solation (II Thess. 2:16,17).

Has some friend disappointed you? One to whom you opened out your
heart? This thing is from Me.

I want to be your Confidant. Has someone repeated things about you
that are untrue? Leave them to Me, and draw closer unto Me, thy
shelter, out of reach of "the strife of tongues" for "I will bring forth thy
righteousness as the light, and thy judgment as the noonday" (Ps. 37:6).

Have your plans been all upset? Are you bowed down and weary? This
thing is from Me. You made your plan, then came asking Me to bless it,
but I would have you let Me plan for you and then I take the responsibility, for, "This thing is too heavy for thee, thou art not able to perform
it thyself alone" (Exod. 18:18). You are only an instrument, not an agent.

Have you longed to do some great work for Me, and instead been laid
aside on a bed of pain and weakness? This thing is from Me. I could not
get your attention in your busy days, and I want to teach you some of My
deepest lessons. "They also serve who only stand and wait."

Some of My greatest workers are those shut out from active service,
that they may learn to wield the weapon of all-prayer.

Are you suddenly called upon to occupy a difficult and responsible
position? Launch out on Me. I am trusting you with the "Possession of
difficulties," and "for this thing the Lord thy God shall bless thee in all
thy works, and in all that thou puttest thine hand unto" (Deut. 15:10).

This day I place in your hand this pot of holy oil, make use of it freely,
My child. Let every circumstance as it arises, every word that pains you,
every interruption that would make you impatient, every revelation of
your own weakness, be anointed with it. Remember, "interruptions are
divine instructions." The sting will go as you learn to see Me in all things.
Therefore, "Set your hearts unto all the words which I testify among you
this day. . .for it is not a vain thing for you; because it is your life, and
through this thing ye shall prolong your days in the land" (Deut. 32:46,
47).

—Laura Barter Snow.

HOW TO HAVE EFFECTIVE DEVOTIONS
By Don & Jessie Sandberg

1. If possible, remove yourself from all distractions. Set your special
time of devotions at a time when the children are more apt to be sleeping
and the telephone is not likely to ring. Having your devotions in the same

chair can sometimes help to prepare your heart for a sweet time of fellowship with the Lord.

2. Avoid the tendency to become sleepy. Five minutes of exercise before you spend time with the Lord will be good for you and it will help to keep you alert. If the room is warm, open a window to bring in fresh air.

3. Pray for an open heart and mind as you read the Word of God. Ask the Lord to help you put all the problems and distresses of the day out of the way until you are ready to deal with them in the perspective of your Bible reading and meditation with Him. Determine that you will obey any commandment or principle which the Lord reveals to you.

4. Keep a "Devotions" book. Systematically keep a record of every prayer request and the date each request was added to your list. Indicate when each prayer was answered. Write down special ideas you get from your reading, new lessons you have learned through some passage of Scripture. This book might also include the words to particular songs and poems which have been a blessing and a constantly growing list of particular verses to be memorized. You might eventually want to add outlines of sermons that have been a special blessing or quotations that will be a help during days of discouragement.

5. Devotions ought to be more than a time of asking God for help in particular needs, even though this is absolutely vital for the Christian. Meditating and enjoying the Lord are experiences that most of us have to learn through practice and patience. We need to learn to hunger for that relationship with Him that can only be compared to what a child feels when he snuggles down into his mother's lap when he needs comforting and love. Private devotions must always include some time reading the Scripture but it probably ought to be the "starting point" rather than the sum of one's own Bible study. Ideally, you will discover some teaching or idea which will excite you enough to make you want to do a more exhaustive study later.

6. Never ever skip your devotional time because you are "too tired to get anything out of it anyway." If you read the Bible and you feel you aren't getting anything, *keep on reading until you find something special that the Lord has planned for you.* Satan will always try to convince you that you are wasting your time. If you are getting bogged down in Jeremiah, stop and read awhile in Psalms or one of the Epistles. The very act of reading the Bible and praying when you don't feel like it is in itself a step of faith and it keeps you in a place where the Lord always has a chance to fix whatever is troubling you.

7. Don't feel bound to one system of study when you read the Bible. Keep trying new ways to learn. Use reference books and supplementary materials when helpful but remember that you do not have to have

"helps" to understand the Bible. The Holy Spirit is your best interpreter.

8. Be very plain and very specific in your praying. If necessary pray out loud so that you will realize exactly what you are asking for. Then: (a) confess your sin and your need for God's help, (b) remind the Lord of His power and your weakness, (c) list past blessings and answers to prayer, (d) praise the Lord even before you see the answer, (e) do exactly what God tells you to do, (f) when the answer comes, let everybody know God has answered prayer.

9. Find something special in your devotions that you can carry with you through the day. If some particular verse is a blessing, write it on a card and tape it over the kitchen sink at home or on the desk at work so that you will see it often. Share your blessings with someone else!

Three important words and three important questions to be asked in the study of any portion of Scripture:

    1. OBSERVATION: What does the passage say?
    2. INTERPRETATION: What does the passage mean?
    3. APPLICATION: What must I do about it today?

Other questions to ask oneself in relation to the passage you are reading:

1. What does this passage tell me about God?
2. What does this passage tell me about Jesus Christ and His work?
3. What does this passage reveal to me about the Holy Spirit and His claim on my life?
4. What does this passage tell me about my sin and how I can avoid it?
5. What does this passage tell me about the Word of God and any promises to claim?
6. What does this passage reveal to me about my heart attitude toward people—specifically, but also generally?

They took away what should have been my eyes,
(But I remembered Milton's Paradise).
They took away what should have been my ears,
(But I had talked with God when I was young).
He would not let them take away my soul,
Possessing that I still possess the whole.
           —Helen Keller.

Did He set you aside
When the fields were ripe
And the workers seemed too few?
Did He set you aside
And give someone else
the task you so longed to do?
Did He set you aside when the purple grapes
hung low in the autumn sun;
And did hands not your own just gather them in—
the trophies you'd almost won?
Did He set you aside on a couch of pain—
There where all you could do was pray;
And then when you whispered, "Oh, please let me go!"
was His answer always, "Stay"?
Did He set you aside with a heavy cross;
and was your heart filled with despair?
Did you think He had gone and left you alone,
then suddenly He was there? And there,
in the shadows, the world all shut out,
just kneeling alone at His feet,
did you learn the answers
(though not all yet)?
Say, weren't His reasons sweet?

—Author unknown.

REFUSE TO LOOK AT SECOND CAUSES

The secret of Hudson Taylor's rest of heart, amid such tempests of hate, was his refusal to look at second causes. His times were in God's hands. He believed that it was with God, and God alone, he had to do. This is strikingly brought out in his article entitled "Blessed Adversity." With the experiences of Job as his text, he wrote:

Even Satan did not presume to ask God to be allowed himself to afflict Job. In the first chapter and the eleventh verse he says: "Put forth Thine hand now, and touch his bone and his flesh, and he will curse Thee to Thy face." Satan knew that none but God could touch Job; and when Satan was permitted to afflict him, Job was quite right in recognizing the Lord Himself as the doer of these things which He permitted to be done.

Oftentimes shall we be helped and blessed if we bear in mind— that Satan is servant, and not master, and that he and wicked men incited by him are only permitted to do that which God by His determinate council and foreknowledge has before determined shall be done. Come joy or come sorrow, we may always take it from the hand of God.

Judas betrayed his Master with a kiss. Our Lord did not stop short at Judas, nor did He even stop short at the great enemy who filled the heart of Judas to do this thing; but He said: 'The cup which my Father hath given Me, shall I not drink it?'

How the tendency to resentment and a wrong feeling would be removed, could we take an injury from the hand of a loving Father, instead of looking chiefly at the agent through whom it comes to us! It matters not who is the postman—it is with the writer of the letter that we are concerned; it matters not who is the messenger—it is with God that His children have to do.

We conclude, therefore, that Job was not mistaken, and that we shall not be mistaken if we follow his example, in accepting all God's providential dealings as from Himself. We may be sure that they will issue in ultimate blessings; because God is GOD, and therefore, "all things work together for good to them that love Him."

A BLUEPRINT FOR BLESSING

1. Give God the first hour of every day.
2. Give God the first day of every week.
3. Give God the first of your income.
4. Give God first consideration in every decision.
5. Give God's Son first place in your heart.

—Source Unknown.

FINDING ANSWERS TO LIFE'S PROBLEMS

A young bride stands in her new kitchen crying into the telephone. The sink is full of dishes, the cat is licking up the milk from a broken pitcher on the floor and bacon is burning in a frying pan on the stove. She sobs into the telephone, "Mother, when is the 'happy-ever-after part' supposed to begin?"

A secretary with her first big job has just discovered that she has mailed contracts to the wrong people, forgotten to remind her boss of his wife's birthday and has made three spelling errors in a letter to the company president. Her boss is furious! She says, in a sad little voice, "My courses in typing and shorthand just didn't cover problems like this!"

The world is made up of so many different kinds of people that it is sometimes hard to find something we all have in common. There is, however, one element of life which we do all share whether we are young or old, rich or poor, educated or uneducated, married or single. We all have problems! Even the child of God, because he is still living in a frail human body and is operating with a fallen nature in a world corrupted and contaminated by sin, has problems.

The difficulties of life, in themselves, are not necessarily bad. In fact, the Christian is commanded in James 1:2-4:

"My brethren, count it all joy when ye fall into divers temptations [or trials]*; Knowing this, that the trying of your faith worketh patience. But let patience have her perfect work, that ye may be perfect and entire, wanting nothing."*

It is our method of handling problems that will bring on either success or failure. Here, for instance, are four methods of dealing with problems that are guaranteed to bring trouble—physically, mentally, socially and spiritually:

1. TURN THE PROBLEM INWARD. Hide it and brood over it. Don't pray about it and don't discuss it with anyone who could help. Let it make you bitter and withdrawn. Develop ulcers. Have a nervous breakdown. Allow yourself to develop a serious mental illness. Let guilt and frustration cut you off from those who love you. By all means, worry!

2. BACK OFF FROM YOUR PROBLEM. Just refuse to face it. Stay away from church so you won't have to recognize your responsibility. Indulge yourself in overeating. Drown your problem in drugs or sleep. Get preoccupied with things, with pleasure. Bury yourself in work to the exclusion of your friends and family. Simply pretend the problem doesn't exist.

3. COMPLAIN ABOUT YOUR PROBLEM. Tell everybody you know what a low blow life has dealt you. Feel sorry for yourself. Indulge your self-pity with bitterness and resentment toward others. Remind yourself and others that no one could possibly understand what you are going through and that nobody cares anyway. Ignore the needs and problems of other people; after all their troubles couldn't possibly be as bad as yours!

4. WORK OUT YOUR OWN PROBLEM WITHOUT REGARD TO OTHER PEOPLE. Climb over other people if you need to, in order to solve your problem. Take authority into your own hands whether God gives it to you or not. Break the law if necessary. Put yourself and your own needs first.

These "solutions to problems" sound ridiculous, don't they, when we see them expressed so callously? But most likely everyone reading these pages today can name someone they know who has tried to find answers to problems in one of the above ways. Maybe we have even identified one of the above responses in our own behavior at some particular time in our lives.

How foolish we are if we refuse to find the answers to our needs in the ways which the Word of God so clearly and wonderfully provides. This is what God says about getting answers to problems:

1. BE TOTALLY SUBMISSIVE TO THE WILL OF GOD. When a problem seems unsolvable, it is often because somewhere along the road we have stepped out of God's will and have started down a path of our own choosing. God cannot reveal His direction for us until we turn our backs on our own stubborn way. Very often the answers come to us clearly and simply when we come to the point where we can say: "Lord, I belong to You. I am Your property and You have a right to do with me whatever You choose. I submit myself to Your will."

When you come to the place of wanting God's will in your life more than any other thing, you will see your problems in a new perspective. You will see solutions you have not recognized before. "He that findeth his life shall lose it; and he that loseth his life for my sake shall find it" (Matt. 10:39).

2. SEARCH THE WORD OF GOD FOR ANSWERS TO YOUR PARTICULAR PROBLEM. Recognize that God knew your special difficulty long before it arose and He has prepared answers in His Word that will help you find solutions. Search for the answers just as diligently as you would search for a valuable piece of jewelry that was lost. As you rest on the Word of God, you will find you are not nearly so upset by some of the situations that have caused you annoyance and grief. The very act of reading and meditating on the Word will make the problems less troublesome. "Great peace have they which love thy law, and nothing shall offend them" (Ps. 119:165).

3. HUMBLY AND FAITHFULLY MEET WITH GOD IN THE CLOSET OF PRAYER FOR ANSWERS TO YOUR PROBLEM. Give God a chance to prove that He can do what He has promised to do.

THE SEVEN-YEAR ITCH: OR HOW TO DECIDE WHEN TO MOVE!

It is probably true that all of us, under particular pressures, in the middle of difficult circumstances, or perhaps feeling somewhat fruitless at specific points in our lives, are tempted to start looking around to see if there is a better situation somewhere else. If we are not careful, we will let influences around us push us out of God's best choice for us, into something "better."

How can a child of God be sure that the decisions being made are, in fact, the will of God? Here are some steps that will help to make decisions clear, and God-ordained:

1. In a time of crisis or decision, the child of God must always pray: "Lord, I am yours and all I have is yours. You have a right to do with me and all I have as You wish. Keep me in the center of Your will and use me for Your glory."

2. Make up your mind that you will not move or change direction without the positive assurance of God's will. Sometimes we are tempted, when frustrated with our present situation, to keep grasping at straws, to try out every possible opportunity without seeking for any guidance from God. Don't do it! Stay steady until God makes His will clear.

3. Don't use your own discomfort or unhappiness as a criteria for finding God's will. Job could hardly have been called "happy" but he was in the center of God's will. When we determine that we will do His will no matter what the cost, then our happiness or unhappiness will not be an issue.

4. Ask yourself: "Do I want an excuse to back away from my problems in this situation? Am I a quitter?"

5. Ask yourself: "Am I reneging on a sacred trust? Will my leaving this responsibility be cheating the investment others have made in me by their prayers, their money, their love, their care for me?"

6. "Is my spiritual condition such that my decisions are reliable?" One who is not committed to do God's will at any cost will not even have the spiritual discernment to see the situation accurately.

7. Ask yourself: "Am I using the opportunities available to me here and now to do God's work, or do I really think the grass is greener on the other side of the fence?" It is always easy to imagine that another situation will provide opportunities for more exciting service for the Lord, better jobs, an easier time paying the bills, more friends, better opportunities for our children, less expensive housing or food costs. Make sure, when you are seeking the Lord's will, that you are not simply looking for an easier way of life.

—Jessie Sandberg.

PEBBLES OF JOY

Dimestore bubble bath
A little teapot
Candles
A bowl of apples
A bunch of wild flowers
A pretty afghan
A letter from an old friend

A baby's wet kiss
A bar of sweet-smelling soap
Sunsets
The song of a mockingbird
A child's laughter
The warm tongue of a puppy
A new box of stationary
Popcorn and cider
A choir singing
A friend's smile
The words, "I love you."
The feel of clean hair
Fall leaves
A crackling log in the fireplace
Rain on the roof at night
A really clever joke
Answered prayer
Rest after pain
The smell of hot bread
A seashell
Something I've made myself
Christmas lights
Victory after the score has been tied
The smell of crayons
Psalm 37
A problem resolved
Sleep when the crisis is over
Colored photographs of the children as babies
Finding a lost earring or glove
A happy ending in a good novel
Finishing something I dreaded doing
Fresh linens on the bed
Birthday cards
A recording of "The Messiah"
The first garden tomato
Remembered lines of favorite poetry
Old love letters
The right answer at the right time
A comfortable old chair
A car that starts on a cold morning
Snowflakes
Meeting someone new
The feel of polished wood

Finding the Bible promise that fits my problem
Hearing a compliment about somebody I love
Introducing someone to the Lord Jesus
Discovering the bitterness is gone.

—Jessie Sandberg.

HOW *NOT* TO TEACH A SUNDAY SCHOOL CLASS

The *wrong* way to teach a Sunday school lesson:

1. Don't bother to prepare; just play it by ear. The kids you teach probably won't know the difference. Just read the quarterly if one is available.

2. Fill up your class time with promotion, extra activities, conversation. Nobody really wants to hear the lesson anyway.

3. Mumble and fidget when you teach. Be sure not to smile; someone may think you actually enjoy teaching the Bible.

4. Ignore the personal needs of your class members; you have your own worries.

5. Saturday night is a good time to start looking over your lesson. Remember you have lots more important things to do than teach a Sunday school lesson!

* * *

The *right* way to teach a Sunday school lesson:

1. Ask the Lord to give you something helpful and practical for yourself in your lesson preparation. If nothing in your reading and study stirs your own heart or convicts you or excites, then those you teach will not be touched and blessed either.

My dad frequently uses this illustration: The Word of God is a sword (Eph. 6:17, Heb. 4:12) but that does not mean it is simply a museum piece to be looked at and admired. It is to be used in the battle for righteousness in a practical and life-changing way.

2. Spend some time in prayer for your individual class members as you prepare the lesson. Ask the Lord to give something for the specific burdens and needs of each of them. (This may mean you will need to take time for prayer requests so that you will know how to pray.) Meeting the needs of your class members does *not* mean you will "pick out" special passages to preach sermons to particular individuals in the class, but you *will* need to ask the Holy Spirit to direct your thoughts and words as you teach, so that the Word will make an impact in each life.

3. Find "nails" to fasten down scriptural messages in the minds of your class members. A simple drawing or diagram on the board may help, a hand-out sheet, object lesson, or a well-thought-out illustration of biblical truth may help. BE FLEXIBLE AND IMAGINATIVE.

4. Develop a burden and a sense of deep responsibility for those to whom you minister in the Sunday school class. Never forget for a moment that you may be the only link between someone in your class and the Lord Jesus Christ.

5. Above all, learn to love your students. Your genuine love for them is more important than your knowledge of the Bible or your gifts as a teacher; in fact, neither of these factors will get to the heart of those you teach unless they are accompanied by love. Ask the Lord to give you a special measure of love for the unlovely—the disinterested, the trouble-maker, the obnoxious, for these are the ones who need you most.

Make the Book live to me, O Lord,
Show me Thyself within Thy Word.
Show me myself, and show me my Saviour,
And make the Book live, to me.

Perhaps They Thought

Perhaps they thought when Christ was born
The world would never know;
Perhaps they thought He's just a child
Like children everywhere.

Perhaps they thought He too will be
A carpenter some day;
And as He played in city streets
They thought Him just a lad.

Perhaps they thought at Cana's feast,
As water turned to wine,
That Christ was just another man
Who knew some clever tricks.

Perhaps they thought as blinded eyes
Were made to see again
That Jesus was a man of worth
And might a teacher be.

Perhaps they thought when Pilate came
And took their Christ away,
That they had somehow been deceived
And must a new Messiah seek.

Perhaps they thought as Jesus died
His life had been in vain,
For they were looking for a king
And now that hope was gone.

And then when Jesus rose again
And death had met defeat:
I wonder what those people thought
Who saw Him live again.

Perhaps you've thought that as you live
You need not Jesus know.
But life outside the Saviour's will
Is only spent in vain.

—Tom Kilpatrick
Used by permission

PRAYER

I got up early in the morning
And rushed right into the day.
I had so much to accomplish
That I didn't take time to pray.

Problems just tumbled around me
And heavier came each task.
I whined, "Why doesn't God help me?"
He said, "You didn't ask."

I groaned and I shouted and I grumbled;
I tried every key in the lock:
I cried, "Why doesn't He open?"
He said, "Son, you didn't knock."

So, I got up early this morning
And paused before entering the day.
I had so much to accomplish
I had to take time to pray.

Anonymous.

I have this on one of the pages in the back of my Bible.

—Mrs. Lee Roberson.

Favorite Recipes --

Old and new

About these recipes. . .

   You will notice that there is not a uniformity in the way they are given. Some are old recipes which I inherited; others were given me by close friends who generously allowed me to include them here. Some were garnered years ago from old magazines and newspapers and through the years have been adapted to the tastes of our family. Some I have copied from yellowed recipe cards from my files and, alas, I know not where they came from. You will notice that some are old favorites and some are more exotic. At our house we love to try lots of new foods and some of the most unusual foods have become our "specialties of the house."

Meats and Main Dishes

HUNGARIAN SAUERKRAUT

1 lb. pork sausage } *brown*
1 onion
5 oz. yellow rice, cooked according to package directions.
#2½ can saurkraut

Grease casserole. Put layer of kraut, rice, then sausage. Repeat, ending with kraut on top. Lightly work ½ pint sour cream into kraut. Bake in 350° F. oven for 1 hour, covered; uncover and bake 15 minutes.

Note: This is good served with Belgian Cucumbers, below:

BELGIAN CUCUMBERS

4 medium cucumbers   *½ tsp. salt*
1 cup yogurt   *1 egg yolk*
½ cup mayonnaise   *fresh dill*

About 20 minutes before serving: (1) Wash and pare cucumbers; cut into ¼" chunks. Cook in boiling salted water 10 minutes or until tender-crisp. (2) Meanwhile beat together yogurt, mayonnaise, salt and egg yolk. Bring almost to a boil. Drain cucumbers, heap on serving dish. Top with sauce. Serve, sprinkled with dill.

Dorys Gagliardi.

RISI E BISI (Luncheon in Milan for 4)

1 small onion, finely chopped
3 TBS. grated Parmesan cheese
½ cup shredded cooked ham
1 pkg. frozen English peas, thawed
3 cups chicken stock
5 TBS. margarine
1½ cups short-grain rice

Saute onion in 2 TBS. margarine. Add ham and peas. Add I cup stock and bring to boil. Add rice and remaining boiling stock. Cook until all stock is absorbed and the rice is just dry but not too soft. Stir in remaining 3 TBS. margarine and the Parmesan cheese.

Sonja North sent this recipe to me right after we returned from a wonderful three weeks in Europe together. She and I both loved the food we were served in Italy and we decided that we were going to start "cooking Italian" when we got home.

BAKED CHICKEN SOUFFLE

(Prepare the night before. Serves 8-10.)

Put slices of Pepperidge Farm bread on bottom of flat baking dish. Cover with large pieces of cooked chicken. Cover with 1 small can sliced water chestnuts. Cover with 1 can mushroom pieces. Beat 3 eggs. Add 2 cups milk. Pour over casserole and let stand 10 minutes. Spread with mayonnaise and cover with 1 cup shredded sharp cheddar cheese. Mix ½ cup celery (cut fine) and ½ cup cream of mushroom soup and one small can sliced pimento. Pour over. Leave in refrigerator overnight.

Bake at 350° for 1½ hours. (Less time in a glass pan.) WATCH!

Hints: Only Pepperidge Farm bread works for this souffle. ½ cup cream of mushroom soup equals ½ can.

Dr. Pauline Ikada.

Pauline is an unusually gifted teacher (married to a biochemist) but she is also a gifted artist and creative cook. The Ikadas entertain a great deal and this is one of the favorites of the dishes they serve. Some people say it tastes even better the next day reheated as leftovers.

CHEESE FLAN

1 medium onion, chopped and sauted in 1 TBS. butter
4 slices dry, broken bread
3 cups milk } *(Soak bread in milk)*
4 eggs beaten
3 slices bacon, fried and crumbled
½ lb. cheese, grated (I combine Swiss and cheddar).
½ tsp. salt
½ tsp. paprika

Combine all ingredients and pour into 2 unbaked pie shells. Bake at 350° for 25 minutes.

Serve with the following sauce:

TOMATO SAUCE

1 can tomato soup, undiluted   *1 3-oz. can of mushroom pieces*
1 cup sour cream   *1 TBS. butter*

Heat all ingredients together just to boiling. Pour over individual servings of flan.

* * *

This was a recipe we were once served in the 16th Century Falcon Hotel in Stratford-upon-Avon in England. (No, I don't really believe the recipe is 400 years old!) When we got home to America, I played around with the recipe, guessing about the ingredients. I believe this is pretty close to the original. At any rate, our family enjoys my version frequently! This is approximately the same dish the French call quiche lorraine.

BAPTIST POT ROAST

The name of this dish came from a family joke. A small daughter of a friend of ours noticed one day that wherever she happened to eat Sunday dinner, she was served pot roast that had been cooking in the oven while the family went to church. One day she asked her mother, "Do all Baptists eat roast beef on Sunday?" Her mother assured her that it wasn't really a religious observance, just a nice way to have dinner ready when you've been in church all morning.

Quickly brown a 3 4 lb Chuck, English or Tip roast in a skillet with 2 TBS. fat, turning once. Put in a large roaster pan with 8 medium potatoes, peeled and quartered, 1 small head of cabbage, quartered, and 8 carrots, peeled and cut in halves. Cover meat with ½ pkg. of dry onion soup mix, and season whole pan with salt, pepper, dashes of Worcestershire sauce and Ac'cent. Mix 1 TBS. Kitchen Bouquet with 1 cup of water and pour over whole.

Cover the roaster pan tightly with aluminum foil and bake at 275-300° for 3 hours.

Ideally, roast should be cooked about ½ hour to the lb. (the books say) but the nice thing about this dinner is that it won't be ruined if the pastor's sermon gets a little long. (So just forget about your dinner and listen to what he has to say!) The nicest thing about this meal is that it smells so good when you walk into the house, and if you've prepared a molded or tossed salad ahead of time you can sit down to the table in just minutes!

FRUIT 'N CHICKEN KABOBS

2 whole broiler-fryer chicken breasts, boned, skinned and cut in 1½"
  pieces
¼ cup corn oil
2 TBS. lemon juice
1 tsp. Ac'cent
½ tsp. salt
1/8 tsp. pepper
1 can (8 oz.) pineapple chunks, drained
12 cherry tomatoes
1 large green pepper, seeded & cut into chunks
1 orange, cut into eighths (or use mandarin orange segments)
¼ cup bottled barbecue sauce
1 12-oz. jar pineapple or peach preserves

Mix together corn oil and lemon juice. Pour over chicken pieces, in a small bowl, and marinate 1 hour. Drain and reserve marinade. Sprinkle chicken with Ac'cent, salt and pepper. Spear chicken chunks on a skewer, alternating with pineapple, tomatoes, pepper and orange.

In a small saucepan, mix together reserved marinade, barbecue sauce and preserves. Heat, stirring constantly, until mixture is blended. Brush kabobs generously with preserve mixture. Place on broiler rack and broil 3 inches from heat for 5 minutes. Turn and brush with preserve mixture. Broil 5 minutes longer.

Makes 4 servings.

* * *

This was a recipe that appeared in our local paper. We found that it adapted well to substitutes and could be used outside on a grill or made in the oven. This is not a complicated recipe but it is pretty, rather "flashy" looking to serve for company.

SHRIMP-CRAB CASSEROLE

1 can crab
2 cans shrimp
1 pt. mayonnaise
2 cups diced celery
1 green pepper cut up
1 med. onion, diced and sauted in 1 TBS. butter
4 hard boiled eggs, chopped
1 cup mushrooms, cut up
1 tsp. salt
1 can water chestnuts, sliced
½ cup almonds (slivered)

Mix all ingredients and put in buttered casserole. Top with buttered crumbs. Bake at 350⁰ for 30 minutes.

POT ROAST INDIENE

4 lbs. lean beef (chuck or round)	4 whole cloves
1 tsp. salt	½ tsp. cinnamon
2 TBS. lemon juice	1 bay leaf
3 slices bacon, fried crisp	1 cup canned tomatoes
1 clove garlic minced	1 tsp. sugar
2/3 cup chopped onion	1 cup orange juice
¼ cup chopped parsley	

Season meat with salt and lemon juice. Cook bacon until crisp; remove from pan. Add meat to bacon drippings. Brown on all sides. Combine garlic, onion, parsley, cloves, cinnamon, bay leaf, tomatoes and sugar. Add to beef. Crumble bacon over meat. Bring to boil; reduce heat and cook until tender. Remove bay leaf and cloves if desired.

SWEET-SOUR PORK

3 lbs. pork (can use regular spare ribs)
1½ tsp. salt
¼ tsp. pepper
1 can (1 lb. 4 oz.) pineapple chunks, drained
2 green peppers, cut in strips
2 TBS. cornstarch
⅓ cup soy sauce
½ cup sugar
¼ cup vinegar

Cover pork with cold water; bring to boil and simmer for 10 min. Drain and rinse in cold water. Place in roasting pan; sprinkle with salt and pepper. Bake in very hot oven (450⁰) for 15 minutes, until lightly browned. Pour off fat. Add pineapple and peppers. Bake 10 minutes. Combine remaining ingredients and juice from pineapple and cook until clear, stirring constantly. Pour over ribs; bake 10 minutes longer.

Makes 6 servings.

PEARL WIEGNER'S CHICKEN CASSEROLE

1 stewing chicken cooked whole—cut up
1 cup chicken soup
1 can mushroom soup
1 can mushrooms cut up
1 can water or chicken broth
1 cup celery cut fine
1 cup onions cut fine
1 can chow mein noodles
1 small package potato chips broken fine

Stir together. Bake 1 hour at 350⁰.

EASY CHICKEN CASSEROLE

Sprinkle: 1 pkg. Lipton's Onion Soup in buttered casserole.
Over that: 1 cup uncooked rice (Minute Rice works too). Lay pieces of uncooked chicken over this and pour over all:

        1 can Cream of Chicken Soup mix with
        2 cans water.

Bake 2 hours at 325⁰ uncovered.

Note: Use shallow casserole such as 9 x 12 or 8 x 15.

GEN'S HAM LOAF

1 lb. ham, ground
1 lb. ground pork
1 cup corn flake crumbs

shape into 1
large or into
individual loaves
(makes about 8).

Bake 1 hour @ 350⁰.

Juice:
¼ cup vinegar
¼ cup water
1½ cup brown sugar
1 TBS. yellow mustard

Baste ham loaf with juice during last half hour of baking.

BAKED WEINERS

Put 1 dozen or more weiners in a baking dish.
Pour over:

1 large can tomatoes
2 TBS. brown sugar⎫ *Blend, mix with tomatoes*
2 TBS. flour ⎭
⅓ Spanish onion—sliced thin
⅓ green pepper, chopped

Bake in moderate oven 2-2½ hours. Serve with cottage cheese and buttered rye slices.

—Pat Sommerlad.

SWEDISH CHICKEN CASSEROLE

Cover bottom of 9 x 13" casserole dish with jar of dried beef. Wrap bacon around 8 deboned chicken breasts and place over dried beef. Mix 1 cup sour cream and 1 can mushroom soup. Pour over chicken. Bake at 275⁰ for 3 hours.

—Carolyn Haskell.

HAM-ASPARAGUS ROLLS

Cut Swiss cheese into fingers. Carefully roll 1 cooked asparagus stalk and one finger of cheese with one thin slice of ham. Place in casserole dish to cover bottom. Pour 1 cup sour cream over the rolls and bake until just warm (10-15 minutes), at 325⁰.

CHEESE RABBIT

2 cups diced sharp Cheddar cheese
2 TBS. flour
1 tsp. dry mustard
½ tsp. salt
1 TBS. margarine
2/3 cup hot milk

Combine all ingredients in blender and whirl at high speed until smooth. Heat in double boiler over simmering water. Good on warm toast, toasted English muffins or crackers. Makes 4 servings.

SPANISH CASSEROLE

3 pkgs. frozen chopped spinach
2 pkgs. (3 oz. each) cream cheese
½ stick butter (divided in half)
Salt, pepper, Ac'cent
Generous dash of nutmeg
Grated rind of one lemon
1 cup of packaged herb bread dressing

Cook spinach according to directions on package. Drain thoroughly. Return to hot sauce-pan and immediately blend in cream cheese and half of the butter. Season with salt, pepper, Ac'cent, nutmeg and lemon rind.

Turn into buttered casserole and refrigerate until ready to bake (45 minutes before baking). Spread dry dressing over top and drizzle with remaining melted butter.

Bake uncovered at 350° for 30 minutes. Serves nine.

—Dotty Allison.

DAGWOOD BUMSTEAD SANDWICHES

¼ lb. American cheese, cubed
3 hard-boiled eggs, chopped
1 - 7 oz. can of flaked tuna, drained
2 TBS. chopped green pepper
2 TBS. chopped onion
2 TBS. stuffed olives, chopped
2 TBS. sweet pickle, chopped
½ cup mayonnaise

Mix lightly, split hamburger buns and fill. Wrap separately in foil and place in a slow oven (250°) about 20-30 minutes until filling is heated and cheese melts. Makes about 8 buns. Serve hot.

Dorothy Carlson   (Moline Free Church).

HOT SANDWICHES

4 cut-up slices bacon
1 small green pepper } *brown together*
1 small onion

1 can tomato) *Add and cook 10 minutes.*
½ lb. hamburger meat } *Cool slightly and put in*
1 cup cubed cheese) *hamburger buns.*

Wrap in aluminum foil and freeze until needed. Heat ½ hour at 300° F. Serve in aluminum foil.

BREAKFAST CASSEROLE

Remove crusts from 5 slices white bread.
grate ½ lb. sharp cheese
Alternate bread and cheese in greased casserole.
Beat 4 eggs slightly with:
2 cups milk
½ tsp. salt
½ tsp. dry mustard

Pour liquid over bread and let set over night. Bake 1 hour at 350⁰. Serve with crumbled bacon on top. Serves 6 to 8.

—Minner Sandberg*

This is a recipe our children loved to have their Aunt Minner fix for them everytime they spent the night at her house. I love to fix it for company because all the work is done the night before. It is a lovely breakfast to serve with coffee, muffins and a fruit cup for guests. It also freezes well but will have to be taken from the freezer the night before or baked for an additional half-hour at 325⁰.

*Those of you who have read the book, *From My Kitchen Window,* will have already met Minner Sandberg in the chapter, "Every Little Girl Should Have an Aunt."

OVEN PANCAKES

3 eggs   *2 TBS. sugar*
2 cups milk   *1 tsp. salt*
1 cup flour

Beat eggs. Add all other ingredients and beat with egg beater till smooth. Pour in heavily greased 8 x 10 pan. Put bacon slices on top. Bake 45 minutes in 425⁰ F. oven. When done, cut into squares and serve with butter and syrup.

(I should be able to tell you how many this recipe will serve but that will depend entirely on the people eating. At our house, the kids just keep on eating until all the food is gone. I have no idea how normal families plan their food production! Just look at your 8 x 10 pan and picture how many you think it will feed.)

By the way, this is another recipe given us by our beloved "Aunt Minner."

BAKED EGGS

This is an excellent dish to serve when you must provide breakfast for a large number of people since all the eggs can be cooked and served at the same time.

Grease muffin tins, allowing one cup for each egg you plan to serve. Fry bacon until almost crisp (again, cooking one piece per egg you plan to serve). Line each muffin-tin cup with pre-cooked bacon and break one egg into each cup. Season with salt and pepper and bake in 350⁰ F. oven until whites are opaque but yokes are still soft. Gently move a knife around the edge of each cup and remove egg onto serving platter. (Allow about 8 minutes for eggs to cook to medium doneness.)

LUMPY PUNCH

1 gallon prepared frozen orange juice
6 bananas sliced
6 oranges, peeled, seeded and cut up
¹⁄₄ cup sugar
small bottle marachino cherries (optional)

This is delicious served for brunch or for your own family at breakfast. You may want to serve it in small cups with spoons.

Breads

GRANDMA SANDBERG'S RYE BREAD

1 cup brown sugar
1 qt. warm water
2 tsp. salt
1 cup lard or bacon drippings, melted
1 cup dark syrup (molasses or Karo)
2 pkgs. dry yeast
3 cups rye flour, stirred
4-6 cups sifted all-purpose flour.

Set yeast in 1 cup of the warm water and the rye flour; let set for 10 minutes. Add sugar, salt, syrup, lard or bacon drippings, and remaining water. Gradually add all-purpose flour until dough can be kneaded on a heavily-floured surface. Place in a greased bowl and brush with melted shortening. Cover and let rise until double (1½ to 2 hours). Punch down and divide into 4 parts (six if pans are small). Let rest for 10 minutes and form loaves. Put into greased pans and let rise until double in bulk (about 1 hour). Bake in 350° F. oven for 35-40 minutes. Cool on rack and brush tops with butter.

NOTE: Grandmother Sandberg was famous for this bread but was never quite able to explain how it was made since her long experience with baking had eliminated her need for measuring. The recipe was acquired when her daughters finally held measuring cups over the bowl to keep track of all the ingredients she "threw" in!

POP-UP BREAD

3 to 3½ cups flour
1 pkg. dry yeast
½ cup milk
½ cup water
½ cup oil
¼ cup sugar
1 tsp. salt
2 eggs
1 cup (4 oz.) grated Cheddar cheese, if desired.

Stir together 1½ cups flour and yeast. Heat milk, water, oil, sugar and salt over low heat only until warm, stirring to blend. Add liquid ingredients to flour-yeast mixture and beat until smooth (about 2 minutes), on medium speed of electric mixer or 300 strokes by hand. Blend in eggs and cheese.

Stir in remainder of flour to make a stiff batter. Beat until batter is smooth and elastic, about 1 minute on med. speed or 150 strokes by hand.

Divide batter into two well-greased one-pound coffee cans. Cover with plastic lids. Let rise in a warm place (80 to 85°) until light and bubbly (about 1 hour). Batter should be about ¼ to ½" below covers. Remove lids.

Bake in preheated 375° F. oven 30 to 35 minutes or until done. Cool in cans 15 minutes before removing.

Note: Spoon flour into dry measuring cup; level. Do not scoop.

BANANA NUT BREAD

½ cup butter or margarine
1 cup sugar
1 egg, beaten
2 cups sifted all-purpose flour
1 tsp. baking powder

½ tsp. baking soda
1 cup mashed bananas
3 TBS. milk
½ cup chopped walnuts

Grease a 9 x 5 x 3-inch loaf pan. Beat butter or margarine, sugar and egg in a large bowl until fluffy. Combine bananas and milk in a bowl. Sift flour, baking powder and baking soda onto wax paper. Stir into sugar mixture alternately with banana-milk mixture. Stir in nuts. Turn into prepared pan. Bake in 350° F. oven 1 hour or until center springs back when lightly pressed with fingertip. Cool in pan on wire rack 5 minutes. Turn out of pan and cool completely.

SOUTHERN SPOON BREAD

There is no way to describe this dish to someone from the North who has never tasted it but it is a lovely, filling addition to any meal—a good substitute for potatoes or rice.

1 cup yellow cornmeal
3 cups milk
1-1½ tsp. salt

2 TBS. butter or margarine
4 eggs, separated

Put first 3 ingredients in heavy saucepan and bring to a boil, stirring. Cook 5 minutes, or until very thick. Add butter and cool, stirring occasionally, to lukewarm. Beat egg whites until stiff but not dry, then beat yolks slightly. Stir yolks into mixture, then fold in whites. Pour into buttered 1½-quart casserole and bake in preheated 400° F. oven 35 minutes, or until firm and lightly browned. Serve at once. Makes 6 to 8 servings.

HONEY CARDAMON BREAD

2 cups milk, scalded
½ cup butter or oleo
2/3 cup sugar
2 TBS. honey
2 tsp. salt
¼ tsp. crushed cardamon seed

1 tsp. cinnamon
2 pkgs. dry yeast
¼ cup lukewarm water
7 cups flour
2 beaten eggs

Combine scalded milk, butter, sugar, honey, salt and spices and cool until lukewarm. Add yeast softened in the lukewarm water. Add beaten eggs and flour and let rise until double in bulk. Punch down and knead lightly. Make braided loaves in greased breadpans (makes 2 large or 3 small loaves). Brush top of loaves with egg (beaten together with 1 TBS. milk) and then sprinkle with finely chopped nuts and sugar. Bake 350° for 35-45 minutes.

Jessie Sandberg.

This is my own version of a Swedish favorite. Because it uses so much yeast it is one of the most "fool-proof" breads you can make. This is one bread that is great served hot (cut with an electric knife, if possible) for a special coffee or tea.

COLONIAL CORN BREAD

1 cup self-rising cornmeal
1/4 cup sugar
2 eggs, beaten

1 cup sour cream
1 cup cream-style corn
1/2 cup bacon drippings

Combine first 5 ingredients, mixing well. Heat bacon drippings in a 10" heavy skillet. Pour all but 2 TBS. of hot drippings into corn meal mixture and mix well. Pour batter into hot skillet and bake at 400° for 30 minutes.

MRS. WILCOX'S BRAN MUFFINS

1-15 oz. box Raisin Bran
1 cup melted oleo
1 cup sugar
4 beaten eggs

1 qt. buttermilk
5 cups flour
5 tsp. soda
2 tsp. salt

Sift flour, soda and salt, add Raisin Bran and mix. Add remainder of ingredients. Bake 15-20 minutes in 400° F. oven.

Soups 'n Salads

PEASANT SOUP*

6 small potatoes, peeled and cut up	
1 carrot cut up	boil together in
1 small onion, chopped and sauted	1 quart of water,
2 chicken bullion cubes	seasoned.

Blend with 2 cups white sauce: 1 stick oleo, ½ cup flour premixed with 3 cups liquid (I use evaporated milk and water for richness). Melt butter in small saucepan, add flour and liquid; stir until thick.

Add:

4-6 slices broken, cooked bacon

1 cup grated cheese (any assorted leftovers will do).

1 TBS. dried parsley

1 TBS. Worchestershire sauce

Assorted seasonings to taste (I use a little garlic salt and seasoned salt and pepper-with-lemon).

1 quarter head cabbage	Chop in blender
1 carrot (this will be your second one)	with 2 cups water.

Add more water as necessary. Soup should be thick. Simmer for about 20 minutes, stirring often. If you have bits of leftover ham or chicken, these could be added.

*Our children named this "Peasant Soup" because I usually made it every Saturday morning, changing the ingredients slightly according to what was available. (I think they thought, too, that any soup made with cabbage was certainly peasant food, although I noticed they always ate heartily!)

When the children were very small I once told them the story of "Stone Soup" and made them a pot, using this recipe, along with one small, smooth, well-scrubbed stone!

The Story of Stone Soup

Once there were two young brothers who had gone out to seek their fortune in the world. They had no money and were very hungry when one hit on a plan to get a good meal in a strange village. When they entered the town the older brother announced to all the women of the village that his younger brother knew a wonderful recipe for making soup out of stones.

The women of the village were thrilled. Just think of all the money they could save if soup could be made of stones! "Please show us your wonderful recipe!" they cried.

"Find a large pot," the younger brother said, "fill it with water and put in five large stones." The ladies of the village immediately found a large pot and began filling it with water while the older brother lit a fire underneath.

Patiently, the younger brother stirred the water while the women of the village watched. Finally he put in a spoon and tasted the "soup."

"Ah, that is very good," he said, "but it still needs something else. Perhaps a potato or two would help the flavor."

"I will get two potatoes," said one housewife running back to her home.

When the potatoes were added, the younger brother continued to stir and then he tasted the soup.

"It is getting better and better," he said, "but I do believe the flavor would be improved if a bit of ham were added."

"I have a ham at my house," another woman said, and with that she hurried home to get it.

When the ham was added the younger brother said, "Now, if only I had a few carrots and onions, I believe this would be the best pot of soup I have ever made."

Very quickly other women ran to get carrots and onions, and soon many other ingredients were added until everybody in the village followed the lovely smell of the great pot of stew cooking.

At last the soup was done and the two brothers each had a large bowl along with every member of the village.

Afterwards the ladies of the village declared that since the two brothers were so clever in making such delicious soup out of stones, they should live in the village and teach the ladies other wonderful things that could be made out of stones!

CHILLED AVACADO SOUP

3 ripe avacados, peeled
  and chopped
1 cup chicken broth
1 cup Half and Half
1 tsp. salt

¼ tsp. onion salt
pinch white pepper
1 tsp. lemon juice
lemon slices

Combine avacado and chicken broth in blender. Blend until smooth. Remove; stir in other ingredients. Cover and refrigerate overnight.

COLD QUICK BORSCHT

1 - 16 oz. can whole beets, undrained
1 - 10 3/4 oz. can chicken broth
1 - 8 oz. carton sour cream
3/4 tsp. salt
1/8 tsp. pepper (white pepper preferred)
1½ tsp. lemon juice
2 TBS. chopped chives

Drain beets, saving liquid. Puree in electric blender. Combine all ingredients except chives and beet liquid. Mix well. Chill. When ready to serve, sprinkle with chives. Serves 4.

POTATO SOUP

6 medium potatoes diced
1 diced carrot
1 cup diced celery (top stalks)
2 tsp salt
3 cups hot water

¼ tsp. marjoram
1 bay leaf
1 tsp. parsley
1 TBS. butter
1 chicken bouillon cube

Cook together until celery is done. Add: 1 slice American cheese or grated cheese, 3 cups milk. Do not boil.

MOLDED FISH SALAD (Main Dish)

1 3-oz. pkg. lemon Jello
1 cup water   } *after syrupy add mayonnaise*
1 tsp. salt
½ lb. cheddar cheese cut in small cubes
3 hard boiled eggs, chopped
1 small can tuna, drained
½ cup mayonnaise   } *blended*
½ cup Half and Half
½ cup chopped nutmeats
3 cups chopped celery

Mix cream/mayonnaise with syrupy Jello and add all other ingredients. Pour into a greased large decorative mold (preferably a fish mold) and place in refrigerator to set.

Unmold carefully on a large platter and decorate with greens and olives.

GREEN STUFF

(No doubt there is a perfectly proper name for this lovely salad but this is what it was called when we were introduced to it, and the name has stuck in our family.)

1 small pkg. lime Jello (use dry)
1 small carton cottage cheese
1 can crushed pineapple, drained
1 medium size tub Cool-Whip (or any other non-dairy whipped topping)
1 cup broken nutmeats

Mix all the ingredients together in a bowl and serve—just as easy as that! Make sure the Jello is evenly mixed throughout the salad. This can be prepared ahead of time, and the leftovers are just as good the next day. Just be sure you stir the mixture slightly before you serve.

Variations: Obviously, you could use strawberry or orange Jello. But then it could hardly be called "Green Stuff." Well, find your own name!

HE-MAN'S SALAD

Slice in layers:
    Lettuce, carrots, celery,
Over each layer sprinkle:
    canned peas
    several dobs mayonnaise
Over whole sprinkle:
    sugar
Let set for a while (about 15 minutes)
    in order to let sugar soak into
    mayonnaise.
Cut several slices of bacon into small pieces and fry crisp. Sprinkle bacon and some fat over whole.
DO NOT TOSS.
Optional: Add shredded cheddar cheese with bacon (about ½ cup).

FROZEN PINEAPPLE SALAD

¼ cup granulated sugar
1 8-oz pkg. cream cheese, softened
¼ cup packed brown sugar
2 cups pineapple-flavored yogurt
1 15¼-oz can crushed pineapple, drained
2 TBS. chopped pecans
2 TBS. chopped red and green candied cherries

In a small mixer bowl, beat together cream cheese and sugars. Stir in yogurt and drained pineapple. Spoon into 10 paper baking cups in muffin pans. Combine pecans and cherries; spoon a little atop each cup. Cover; freeze firm. Let stand 10 minutes before serving. Makes 10 servings.

PEANUT-APPLE SALAD

3 cups diced unpeeled red apples   *½ cup mayonnaise*
1 cup diced celery   *3 TBS. honey*
3/4 cup salted peanuts   *1 tsp. celery seed*

Put first 3 ingredients in bowl. Mix remaining ingredients, except greens, and pour over mixture. Stir to coat and serve on greens, if desired. Makes 6 servings.

"Too many girls think a woman's work is done when she sweeps down the aisle."
—**Frances Benson** in *Family Weekly*

HOT GERMAN POTATO SALAD

6 medium potatoes—boiled in
  jackets, peeled and sliced
6 slices bacon, fried slowly
3/4 cup chopped onions
2 TBS. flour
1 to 2 TBS. sugar

1½ tsp. salt
dash of pepper
½ tsp. celery seed
3/4 cup water
1/3 cup vinegar

Saute onions. Use ¼ cup of bacon fat for sauce; add water and vinegar last. Boil one minute. Carefully add sliced potatoes and diced bacon.

Remove from heat; cover and let stand until ready to serve. 6-8 servings.

CINNAMON APPLE SALAD (Molded)

Boil together 1 cup water, ¼ cup sugar, and 4 TBS. red cinnamon candies. When candies are dissolved, cook 2 medium apples, which have been cored, pared and sliced, in cinnamon syrup until red and tender.

Prepare 1 pkg. (3 oz.) of any red-colored Jello using cinnamon syrup as part of liquid. Add apples and 1 cup diced celery. Any other fruit, such as crushed pineapple or bananas may be added according to personal taste.

MRS. HARRINGTON'S SALAD DRESSING

1 can tomato soup
1¼ cup Mazola oil
3/4 cup vinegar
3/4 cup sugar
2 tsp. paprika

1 tsp. salt
1 tsp. dry mustard
1 tsp. onion grated
1 tsp. celery seed

Put all ingredients in a big bottle and shake well. Makes about a pint and a half of dressing.

RUSSIAN DRESSING

½ cup condensed tomato soup
1/3 cup white vinegar
3/4 cup salad oil
½ small clove garlic
½ small onion

½ cup sugar
1 TBS. dry mustard
1 TBS. salt
1 TBS. Worcestershire sauce
½ tsp. paprika

Put all ingredients in blender and process until well blended. Yield: about 2 cups.

This is a wonderfully quick recipe to prepare, just a little sweeter than commerical dressings and very tasty. It keeps in the refrigerator for a long time, unless your family happens to gobble it up very fast as mine usually does!

MINNER'S CHILI SAUCE

12 large tomatoes (peeled)
4 apples
4 onions   } Grind
4 red sweet mango peppers (or green)

Cook with:
3 cups sugar
3 cups white vinegar
1 tsp. whole allspice
1 stick cinnamon broken } tie in cloth
salt to taste (about 1½ TBS.)
Makes 4 pints.

BLENDER HOLLANDAISE

3 egg yolks, at room temperature
1 TBS. lemon juice
Few grains cayenne pepper
½ cup melted butter or margarine
2 TBS. milk (optional)

Place egg yolks, lemon juice and cayenne in the container of an electric blender. Mix at high speed for 20 seconds, or until thoroughly combined and frothy. Reduce speed to medium and gradually add the melted butter while the blender is on. Continue beating until thick and frothy. If sauce is too thick, add milk until the desired consistency. Sauce may be made ahead. Store covered in the refrigerator. To use, set the container in warm water; stir until a consistency for dipping. Makes about 3/4 cup.

GREEN GODDESS DRESSING

1 clove garlic, grated or put through a garlic press
2 TBS. finely chopped anchovies or anchovy paste
3 TBS. finely chopped chives or green onion
1/3 cup finely chopped or dried parsley
1 TBS. lemon juice
3 TBS. tarragon wine vinegar (plain will do)
½ cup dairy sour cream
1 cup mayonnaise
Salt and pepper to taste

Combine all ingredients and chill until needed.

Even
Vegetables

BROCCOLI AND RICE CASSEROLE

½ stick margarine
½ cup chopped celery
½ cup chopped onion
1 cup rice (cook with 2 cups water)
1 can cream of chicken soup

1 can cream of mushroom soup
1 cup grated cheese
1 pkg. frozen chopped broccoli
*   (cooked and drained)*
½ tsp. salt

Cook rice. Cook broccoli and drain. Mix all ingredients in mixing bowl. Pour into 9 x 13 casserole and cook. Bake at 350° about 30 minutes.

Sue Erickson.

Don't fix a fancy meat dish when you serve this casserole. It is rich enough and has enough protein for you to skip the meat altogether if you wish. If you are serving it for company (nice for a lunch or buffet), you may want to serve thin slices of ham rolled up and pinned with a toothpick, served cold. Some fruit salad and dainty rolls would polish off this meal nicely!

SQUASH CASSEROLE

4-6 yellow squash } *cook slightly*
2 onions
1 cup shredded cheddar cheese
½ cup slivered almonds
2 eggs, beaten
2 tsps. sugar

Mix all ingredients. Place in greased casserole dish. Cover with cracker crumbs. Bake 45 minutes at 300°.

* * *

Pastor's wives, it seems, are always avid collectors of good recipes. My sister, Grace MacMullen, got this recipe in one of the churches where her husband served as pastor and when she gave it to me, Grace called it, "Byrle's Squash casserole."

SPINACH CASSEROLE

3 pkgs. frozen chopped spinach
2 (3 oz.) pkgs. cream cheese
¼ cup butter (divide in half)
salt, pepper, Ac'cent
generous dash nutmeg
grated rind of one lemon
1 cup of packaged herb bread dressing

Cook spinach according to directions on package. Drain thoroughly. Return to hot saucepan and immediately blend in cream cheese and half of the butter. Season with salt, pepper, Ac'cent, nutmeg and lemon rind.

Turn into buttered casserole and refrigerate until ready to bake (45 minutes before serving). Spread dry dressing over top and drizzle with remaining melted butter.

Bake uncovered at 350° for 30 minutes. Serves 9.

—Dotty Allison.

CREAMED ASPARAGUS AND CARROTS

Cook one package of frozen asparagus and one bunch of carrots. Make one cup of thick cream cheese sauce. Place in alternate layers in casserole and bake in 350° F. oven for 30 minutes.

—Alice Sandberg.

RICE BALLS

Beat one large egg slightly and add 2 cups cooked rice, 5 TBS. fine dry bread crumbs, 2 TBS. each of chopped parsley and pimiento, 1 minced small onion, and salt and pepper to taste. Form into 12 small balls and chill. A half hour before the chicken is done, arrange the balls in a ring around the edge of a casserole. Baste with gravy at least twice.

ITALIAN EGGPLANT PARMIGIANA

¼ cup vegetable oil	½ tsp oregano leaves
1 cup chopped onion	½ cup wheat germ
1 clove garlic, minced	1/3 cup fine, dry bread crumbs
1 can (1 lb.) tomatoes	1 eggplant, about 1½ lbs.
1 can (8 oz.) tomato sauce	2 eggs, beaten
1 tsp. salt	1/3 cup vegetable oil
1 tsp. sugar	1 pkg. (6 oz.) sliced mozzarella cheese
½ tsp. basil leaves	¼ cup grated Parmesan cheese

A 2-qt. saucepan, heat ¼ cup vegetable oil, add onion and garlic. Saute until golden, about 8 minutes. Stir in undrained tomatoes, tomato sauce, ½ tsp. salt, sugar, basil and oregano. Bring to boiling and cover. Reduce heat and simmer for 20 minutes. Break up tomatoes if still whole. On wax paper, combine wheat germ, bread crumbs and ½ tsp. salt. Cut eggplant crosswise into ½-in. slices. Dip in beaten egg, then in wheat-germ mixture, coating both sides. Heat 1/3 cup oil in large skillet, cook eggplant in single layer over medium heat about 2½ minutes per side until coating is golden. Drain on paper towels.

Preheat oven to 400° F. Pour half of tomato sauce in shallow 2-qt. casserole. Layer overlapping slices of eggplant in sauce. Cover with cheese slices; top with sauce and sprinkle with Parmesan cheese. Bake for 20 to 30 minutes until hot and bubbly.

VEGETABLE WHIP

4 medium potatoes, cubed
4 medium carrots, sliced
1 small onion chopped
1 tart apple, pared and sliced

1 cup boiling water
4 TBS. salad oil
1 tsp. salt
4 TBS. cream

Combine vegetables, apple, water, salad oil and salt and cover and simmer until tender. Remove cover and stir until water has evaporated. Mash. Add cream. Beat until light and fluffy. Very good with fresh side pork or pork roast.

—Minner Sandberg.

Family Favorite Cakes

HOW TO BAKE A CAKE (HOPEFULLY!)

Light oven; get out bowls, spoons, and ingredients. Grease pan, crack nuts. Remove 18 blocks and 7 toy cars from kitchen table.

Measure out 2 cups of flour; remove Johnny's hands from the flour and wash the flour off Johnny.

Put flour, baking powder, salt in sifter. Get dustpan and brush up pieces of bowl that Johnny knocked off the table and onto the floor. Get another bowl. Answer doorbell.

Return to kitchen. Remove Johnny's hands from bowl. Wash Johnny. Get out eggs. Answer phone. Return. Take out greased pan. Remove ½-inch salt from pan. Find Johnny.

Return to kitchen and find Johnny; remove his hands from bowl; wash shortening, etc., off him. Take up greased pan and remove ½-inch layer of nutshells. Head for Johnny (who in fleeing has knocked bowl off table.)

Wash kitchen floor; wash table; wash walls; wash dishes. Call up the baker. Lie down. (I add—1 switch to Johnny and a prayer.)

—Source unknown.

COLONIAL POUND CAKE

1 cup butter
(1 stick butter and 1 stick oleo will produce a lighter cake.)
1 2/3 cups sugar
2 cups cake flour (sift 5 or 6 times)
5 eggs
1½ tsp. vanilla

Cream until the consistency of whipped cream the butter and sugar. Add eggs one at a time, beating well after each addition. Add vanilla after last egg, beating well. Fold in flour. Bake in well greased and floured 9" tube pan in a 325° F. oven for 1½ hours or until tests done. (P.T. says hers are done in 1 hour; mine were done in 50 minutes: J.S.)

Peggy Titsworth.

At our house, we love to prepare "theme" dinners. We have had Chinese dinners with the unopened folding table propped a foot off the floor with books while we sat on cushions to eat. We have had spaghetti suppers on homemade checkered-clothed tables with candles in bottles.

One of our nicest memories is of the "Colonial dinner" the children made using old, authentic colonial recipes. This was one affair in which we adults were the guests of honor and we enjoyed it tremendously (even after we had voluntarily cleaned up a disastrously messy kitchen in which the dinner was produced!)

Here is a nice, not-too-complicated cake recipe your children can use just in case they get in a mood to do a Colonial meal (and assuming you trust them to knock around in your kitchen and china cupboard)!

7-UP POUND CAKE

CREAM:

2 *sticks margarine (or butter)*	3 *cups plain flour*
½ *cup Crisco*	3/4 *cup 7-Up*
3 *cups sugar*	1 *tsp. vanilla*
5 *eggs (extra large)*	1 *tsp. lemon flavoring*

Alternate flour and 7-Up, beat well. Add flavoring. Bake 45 minutes at 350°, reduce heat to 300° and continue baking for 35 minutes. Cool and remove from pan.

Note: Grease pan (angel food tube pan) and dust with flour.

I know this recipe distinctly says, "Cool and remove from pan" but at our house we like to get it out of the pan just as soon as it can be safely taken out without squashing together or falling apart. Then we eat it hot with ice cream. Delicious!

OUT-OF-THIS-WORLD CAKE

Cream together:

½ *lb. margarine*

2 *cups sugar*

Add, beating well after each:

6 *eggs, one at a time*

Alternate and add:

½ *cup milk*

8 *oz. vanilla wafers, finely ground*

Add:

7 *oz. coconut*

1 *cup coarse pecans*

Bake in a tube pan only, in 300° F. oven for 1½ hours.

SPICE APPLE CAKE

1 *box Duncan Hines Spice Cake*

1 *can Apple pie mix (finely cut)*

Mix eggs and cake mix together and add apples. Mix well. Bake in greased and floured tube or oblong pan at 350° for 1 hour. Frost with white frosting mix.

•   —Judy Sligev.

This is a rich, fruity cake that stays moist a long time. You may find you enjoy it as much (or more) without the frosting. This one really needs to cool well before you cut it.

SOCK-IT-TO-ME CAKE

1 box Duncan Hines (Butter Supreme) yellow cake mix
½ cup sugar
4 eggs
3/4 cup oil

2 tsp. vanilla
1 pkg. sour cream
1 cup broken nuts (I use pecans)

Preheat oven to 325-350° F. Mix all ingredients except nuts together and beat until smooth. Add nuts and pour half of batter into well-greased tube pan. Sprinkle on mixture of 1 TBS. dark brown sugar and 1 TBS. cinnamon. Pour remainder of batter in pan and bake for 1 hour or until cake tests done. (50 minutes may be long enough.)

Regina Siler, the hostess extraordinary who gave me this recipe, says: "I usually use wax paper on the bottom of the pan. I also let it cool almost completely before removing from pan."

PISTACHIO GREEN CAKE

1 box Duncan Hines Golden Butter Cake Mix
*1 box Pistachio **instant** pudding mix*
4 eggs

1 cup sour cream
½ cup Crisco oil

Mix all ingredients together until well blended. Pour half of batter in ungreased Bundt or angel cake pan. Sprinkle with half nut mixture. Pour in remaining batter. Sprinkle with remaining nut mixture on top.

Do not preheat oven. Bake at 350° F. for one hour or until toothpick comes out clean. Cool completely before removing from pan.

NUT MIXTURE:

Mix together:

½ cup chopped nuts (pecans)

1 TBS. sugar
1 tsp. cinnamon

Kathy Underwood.

Variations of this recipe have been very popular in our town this year. This is a nice fool-proof kind of recipe for a beginning cook who wants to make a good impression! Kathy Underwood, who claims to be a "non-cook," really wowed her family when she brought this to the Thanksgiving dinner!

PLUM GOOD CAKE

3 large eggs
2 cups sugar
2 cups self-rising flour
1 cup Wesson Oil

1 tsp. ground cloves
1 tsp. cinamon
2 small jars plum baby food
1 cup pecans or black walnuts

"Dump" all ingredients into large mixing bowl. Beat until well mixed. Pour into well-greased tube pan and bake 1 hour at 350°.

—Peggy Titsworth.

I just couldn't resist adding one recipe made out of baby food. What will they think of next?

CHEWIE CAKE

1 stick melted oleo
2 cups light brown sugar
1 tsp. vanilla
Beat in 2 eggs
Add 2 cups self-rising flour
1 cup nuts (cut small)

Spread in 9 x 14 pan which has been well-greased or lined with wax paper. Bake at 325° for 20 to 25 minutes.

CRUNCH CAKE

2 cups sugar
2 cups plain flour
6 eggs
½ cup margarine
½ cup Crisco

1 cup milk
1 tsp. vanilla extract
1 tsp. almond extract
½ cup chopped nuts (optional)

Beat for 12 minutes. Start with a cold oven.* Bake at 300° for 40 minutes; 325° for an additional 20 minutes.

*Pour into well-greased tube pan.

—Renee Ellenwood.

MEGEVE CAKE

(A famous dessert served at Fauchon's on Rue Madeleine, Paris)
Meringue:
3 egg whites
1 cup (less 1 TBS.) granulated sugar

Whipped Chocolate Filling:
2/3 cup heavy cream
7 squares (1 oz. each) semisweet chocolate
3½ squares (1 oz. each) unsweetened chocolate
4 TBS. butter or margarine
4 egg whites
1 cup (less 1 TBS.) granulated sugar

Grease 2 cooky sheets (1 large and 1 small) and dust with flour. Using an 8" layer cake pan draw 2 circles on large cookie sheet and one on small. Beat 2 egg whites until foamy-white and double in volume. Sprinkle in 1 cup (less 1 TBS.) sugar SLOWLY, beating all the time until sugar is dissolved and meringue stands in firm peaks. Spoon evenly into the 3 circles, spread to edge. Bake in slow oven (300°) 30 minutes or until layers are firm and lightly golden. Cool 5 minutes and then loosen layers carefully with a wide spatula and slide onto racks; cool.

MAKE CHOCOLATE CURLS: Melt 7 squares semisweet chocolate in a small bowl over hot water. Turn out onto cold cookie sheet and spread to a 6" x 4" rectangle. Refrigerate until just set. Pull a long metal spatula across chocolate, letting the soft chocolate curl up in front of spatula. Place on wax paper and cool.

MAKE FILLING: Heat cream in top of a double boiler; add semi and unsweetened chocolate. Stir and add butter. Beat 4 egg whites until foamy-white with electric mixer; gradually add remaining sugar, beating until meringue is glossy and stands in firm peaks. Set aside. Fill bottom of double boiler partly with ice and water; set top of boiler with chocolate mixture in ice water. Beat at high speed with electric mixer until light and fluffy and almost double in volume. Scrape down sides often. Fold chocolate into meringue until no streaks remain.

Place 1 meringue layer on serving plate; spread with about 1½ cups filling; repeat with another layer and ½ cup filling. Place 3rd layer on top. Frost sides and top with remaining filling. Pile chocolate curls on top and side. 30 minutes before serving remove cake from refrigerater and sprinkle with powdered sugar. Cut in wedges with sharp scissors.

*This is a very fancy recipe that requires strict following of instructions. Since we do not like things *very* sweet at our house I cut down the sugar in both meringues and filling to 2/3 cup.

All Kinds Of Pies

CHOCOLATE SUNDAE PIE

Crush: 18 cream-filled chocolate cookies (Oreos) to fine crumbs with rolling pin and
Add: 1/3 cup melted butter or margarine. Mix well and press in 9" pie pan. Chill.
Melt: 2 sqs. (2 oz.) unsweetened chocolate over hot water and stir in ½ cup sugar and 1 TBS. butter or margarine.
Add: 1 small can (2/3 cup) evaporated milk, slowly.

Cook over hot water stirring occasionally until thick. Chill. Fill pie shell with ice cream (vanilla) and spread chocolate mixture over the top. Whip cream and spoon over the surface of pie. Sprinkle with walnuts. Serve at once or store in freezer. Serves 6.

Variation: Make crust with vanilla wafers instead of Oreos. Use a box of frozen strawberries as a substitute for chocolate mixture. (Thaw and pour on top of ice cream and return to the freezer before covering with whipped cream and nuts.)

This dessert can be doubled and made in a 9" x 13" pan to serve 12.

Minner Sandberg.

This is one of the "most favorite" desserts at our house. I always make big batches of it when I serve it for company and then we keep any leftovers (covered with foil) in our freezer for our family to enjoy afterward.

JAPANESE FRUIT PIE

2 eggs beaten
1 cup sugar
1 stick oleo
½ tsp. vanilla

½ tsp. vinegar
½ cup pecans
½ cup coconut
½ cup raisins

Mix sugar and melted oleo. Add to eggs; mix well. Add vinegar, vanilla, nuts, raisins, coconut. Pour into pie shell and bake for 50 minutes at 350° F. Do not refrigerate.

Now if you like rich and fancy desserts, you will love this one! Don't make it if you are counting calories and cut your pieces small. I think it tastes better served with whipped cream (doesn't everything?).

—Peggy Titsworth.

CRUSTLESS CHESS PIE

1 cup sugar
½ cup brown sugar (light)
1 stick butter or oleo
3 eggs slightly beaten
1 TBS. vinegar

2 TBS. cream or milk
1 tsp. vanilla
Add pecans, if desired

This recipe, a favorite one in Tennessee, was adapted by my mother, Mrs. John R. Rice, to suit the special tastes of my dad. Mother says: "I butter my pie pan and bake it without any crust. It comes out fine in wedges."

Bake 30 minutes in 325° F. oven.

Since this is a very rich dessert, you might want to serve it with whipped cream, slightly sweetened.

PUMPKIN CHIFFON PIE

1 envelope unflavored gelatin
1 cup sugar (divide into 2 half-cups)
½ tsp. each of ginger, nutmeg and cinnamon
½ tsp. salt
3 eggs separated
3/4 cup milk
1½ cups canned pumpkin
1 baked 9" pie shell

In the top of a double boiler stir together gelatin, ½ cup sugar, spices and salt. Add egg yolks, milk and pumpkin. Cook over boiling water for 10 minutes, stirring constantly, or until thick. Remove from heat and chill until mixture begins to stiffen. Beat egg whites until almost stiff, and then gradually add remaining ½ cup sugar and beat until stiff. Fold into pumpkin mixture and pour into shell. Chill until firm.

LEMONADE PIE

Make graham cracker crust:
Mix: 1¼ cups packaged graham cracker crumbs
¼ cup sugar
¼ cup softened butter.

Pour into 9" piepan. Press firmly against bottom and sides of pan. Bake in preheated 375° F. oven about 8 minutes.

Mix filling:
1 can (14 oz.) sweetened condensed milk (not evaporated)
1 can (6 oz.) frozen pink lemonade
Juice of 1 large lemon
1 carton (9 oz.) frozen whipped topping, thawed.

Mix all ingredients and pour into crust; chill.

KENTUCKY HIGH DAY PIE

1 9-inch unbaked pastry shell
2 eggs
1 cup sugar

½ *cup butter or margarine, melted*
1 *tsp. vanilla*
¼ *cup cornstarch*
1 *cup finely chopped pecans*
1 *cup (6 oz. pkg.) semi-sweet chocolate chips OR 1 cup (5-3/4 oz. pkg.)*
  milk chocolate chips

In a small mixer bowl, beat eggs slightly; gradually add sugar. Add melted butter or margarine and vanilla. Mix well. Blend in cornstarch. Stir in pecans and chocolate chips; pour into unbaked pastry shell. Bake at 350⁰ F. for 45-50 minutes. Cool 1 hour and serve warm with a dollop of whipped cream.

NOTE: This pie freezes well. To serve, remove from freezer and warm at 300⁰ F. for 35-40 minutes.

BUTTERMILK PIE

3 *eggs*
1½ *cups sugar*
pinch salt
1 *TBS. flour*
½ *cup buttermilk*
1 *tsp. vanilla*
1 *stick melted margarine*

Beat eggs well; add other ingredients and mix until thoroughly blended at low speed on mixer (do not overbeat). Pour into unbaked piecrust shell. Bake 1 hour at 350⁰ F.

MILLION DOLLAR PIE

1 *can sliced peaches*
1 *can crushed pineapple*
1 *can mandarin oranges*
1 *can sweetened condensed milk (not evaporated)*
1 *large carton frozen whipped topping, thawed*
¼ *cup lemon juice*
1 *cup chopped pecans*
2 *prepared vanilla wafer crusts*

Drain all fruit well. Cut fruit into small pieces. Mix lemon juice and milk. Add all other ingredients and put into prepared pie shells. Decorate top with additional pecan halves and refrigerate overnight. Makes 2 pies.

Cookies

...for special occasions and special people!

SUGAR COOKERY

She measured out the butter with a very solemn air,
The milk and sugar also; and she took the greatest care
To count the eggs correctly, and to add a little bit
Of baking powder, which, you know, beginners oft omit;
Then she stirred it all together; and
She baked it full an hour;
But she never quite forgave herself
For leaving out the flour!

—Author Unknown.

CONGO SQUARES

2-3/4 cups self-rising flour
2/3 cup shortening
1 box light brown sugar
3 eggs
1 large pkg. chocolate chips
½ to 1 cup chopped pecans

Melt shortening and mix with sugar, add eggs one at a time, add flour, nuts and chips. Batter will be sticky! Spread in a greased 9" x 12" pan. Cook 25-30 minutes at 350°. Let cool before cutting.

Pat Taylor.

This is a variation of a brownie recipe that has a bit of a butterscotch taste (because of all that brown sugar). These don't cut too neatly but I can almost guarantee that all the little bodies hovering around the oven waiting for them to finish baking, really will not mind!

POTATO CHIP COOKIES

1 cup oleo
½ cup sugar
1 egg yolk
1 tsp. vanilla

1½ cups flour
½ cup crushed potato chips
½ cup nut meats

Cream butter and sugar. Add egg yolk and rest of ingredients. Drop by tsp. on greased cookie sheet. Bake at 350° about 10 minutes.

Myrt Anderson (Don's Aunt).

This recipe, given me by my husband's fantastic Aunt Myrt, is going to surprise you. It is unusually rich and light—very delicate—the kind of cookie you will serve at a nice tea or formal occasion. It is such a fragile cookie that you will need to store (or freeze) carefully. It "re-crisps" in the oven very nicely just in case you manage to have any around long enough to find out!

JULSTERNER

Christmas Stars from Sweden

½ cup butter
1/3 cup sugar
½ tsp. vanilla
1 egg yolk

1¼ cups sifted flour
½ tsp. salt
½ tsp. baking powder
1 egg white, slightly beaten

Filling: Mix 1/3 cup chopped walnuts with 2 TBS. sugar.

Heat oven to 375° F. Cream butter with sugar and vanilla till fluffy. Beat in egg yolk. Sift dry ingredients into mixture, blending well. Chill one hour or more.

To form stars: Roll 1/8" thick; cut into 2½" squares. Place on cookie sheet, brush with egg white. Cut each corner diagonally almost to center; sprinkle with spoonful filling. Fold every other point to center forming star. Bake 5-6 minutes. Cool. Top with strawberry jam if desired. Makes 2 dozen cookies.

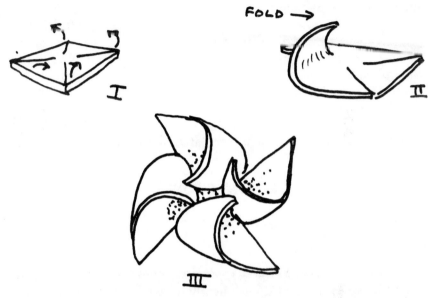

MINT-TOP BROWNIES

To make brownies:

½ cup shortening

2 1-oz. squares unsweetened chocolate

2 eggs

1 cup sugar

1 tsp. vanilla

3/4 cup sifted plain flour

½ tsp. baking powder

½ tsp. salt

1 cup broken nutmeats

(optional)

Melt shortening and chocolate together over very low heat, stirring constantly; cool. Beat eggs till light; stir in sugar, then chocolate mixture and vanilla. Add sifted dry ingredients, mixing well. Add nuts.

Bake in greased 13 x 9 x 2-inch pan at 350° for 25 minutes. Cool.

To make frosting:*

1 cup sugar

1/3 cup water

¼ tsp. cream of tartar

dash salt

1 egg white

¼ tsp. vanilla

*May be tinted pink with 3 drops red food coloring

Bring sugar, water, cream of tartar, and salt to a boil; cook till sugar dissolves.

Slowly add to unbeaten egg white, beating constantly with electric or rotary beater till of spreading consistency. Add vanilla. Spread on top of cooled brownies. Coarsely crush hard peppermint candy to make ½ cup. Sprinkle on top frosting. Cut into 40 pieces.

GINGER COOKIE BALLS

1 cup sugar   2½ cups flour
3/4 cup butter   dash salt
1 egg   1 tsp. ginger
4 TBS. molasses   1 tsp. cinnamon
2 tsp. soda   ½ tsp. cloves

Roll in small balls and dip in granulated sugar before baking. Bake at 350°.

COCONUT CONES

¼ cup butter or margarine
2½ cups sifted confectioner's sugar
¼ cup evaporated milk
3 cups flaked coconut
1 6-oz. pkg. (1 cup) semi-sweet chocolate chips

Melt butter over low heat until lightly browned. Stir in confectioner's sugar, evaporated milk and coconut. Drop from teaspoon onto a waxed paper lined cookie sheet. When cool shape into cones. Melt chocolate chips and dip bottom of cones into melted chocolate; return to waxed paper until chocolate hardens.

Recipe from old magazine, unidentified.

ENGLISH NUT BARS

3/4 cup (1½ stick) butter   1 3/4 cups sifted flour
3/4 cup sugar   ½ tsp. salt
1 egg yolk   1 egg white
1 tsp. vanilla   3/4 cup chopped nuts

In a mixing bowl cream butter; gradually add sugar and beat until light and fluffy. Beat in egg yolk and vanilla. Sift together flour and salt; gradually add to creamed mixture. Spread evenly in 13 x 9 x 2-inch baking pan; brush top lightly with egg white and sprinkle with nuts. Bake in a preheated oven 325° for 30-35 minutes. Cool slightly in pan on wire rack; cut into 1-inch bars or diamonds. Cool completely before removing bars from pan.

Makes 40 bars.   Recipe from *Moline Dispatch*, Christmas 1972.

SWISS CRISPS

1 cup softened butter
1 cup sugar
1 egg yolk
1 TBS. grated semi-sweet chocolate
¼ tsp. salt

1¼ tsp. cinnamon
1 TBS. almond extract
2½ cups all-purpose flour
½ tsp. baking powder
finely chopped almonds (optional)

Cream butter and sugar, using electric mixer, if available. Add egg yolk, chocolate, salt and ¼ tsp. (only) cinnamon. Add extract, flour and baking powder. Mix with hands until dough holds together. It will be soft, so chill until firm enough to roll. Roll very thin, using a small amount of dough at a time. Cut into fancy shapes. Transfer to cookie sheet, allowing ½-in. between cookies. Sprinkle with a mixture of 2 TBS. sugar and remaining cinnamon or with almonds. Bake in moderate oven (350⁰) 10 to 12 minutes or until lightly browned. Loosen at once with a pancake turner and let stand until cool. Store airtight. These cookies make fine escorts for ice cream.

Makes about 12 dozen small cookies.

Recipe from *Women's Day*, Christmas, 1966.

NO-BAKE FRUIT JUMBLES

1 TBS. butter or margarine
½ cup chopped dried apricots
1 egg
½ cup sugar
½ tsp. vanilla

¼ cup chopped nuts
¼ cup shredded coconut
½ cup graham cracker crumbs
(finely crushed)

Melt butter in skillet over low heat. Add apricots and stir. Beat eggs well, and add sugar and eggs to fruit mixture in skillet. Cook over low heat for 10 minutes, stirring occasionally. Remove from heat. Stir in vanilla, nuts, coconut, and graham cracker crumbs. Drop by teaspoonfuls onto waxed paper. Let stand until set.

Recipe from Carol Sandberg.

PECAN TUSSIES

½ cup butter
1 3 oz. pkg. cream cheese
1 cup flour

Mix like piecrust and spread into small muffin tins.

Filling:

2 eggs slightly beaten
1½ cup brown sugar

2 TBS. melted butter
½ cup chopped pecans

Mix and fill crust almost to top. Bake 350° for 16 minutes, 250° for 10 minutes. Makes 26-28 cookies.

Recipe from Alice Sandberg.

PEANUT BUTTER SQUARES

3 cups Special K
1 cup crunchy peanut butter

½ cup sugar
½ cup white Karo

Heat together until melted. Mix with Special K.
Pat mixture into 8 x 13" pan (greased). Sprinkle with 6 oz. pkg. of chocolate chips. Put in 300° oven until chips are melted Spread with knife. Cool and cut into squares.

GLACE LACE COOKIES

½ cup softened butter
2 cups packed dark brown sugar
2 eggs

3/4 cups all-purpose flour
2 tsp. baking powder
½ tsp. salt

Cream butter with sugar, using fingers. Beat in eggs, one at a time and stir in flour, baking powder and salt. Spread foil on cookie sheets and butter lightly. Drop dough onto foil by measuring half tsp. 2 inches apart. Bake in hot oven (400°) 4 to 5 minutes or until cookies are caramel-brown. When cookies seem done, remove from oven and lift one with pancake turner. If cookies stick to foil, put back in oven. Do not try to remove cookies while hot.
Place at once in refrigerator and chill 5 minutes, or until thoroughly cooled, then peel off from foil. Use foil again and again until all dough is used. (No need to butter again.) Keep 2 pans going at once, putting one in the oven as soon as the other is removed.
Makes about 18 doz. cookies.
(A variation on this recipe is to add 2 cups finely chopped pecans to the flour and then blend with the fingers into the butter-egg mixture. Bake as directed. Makes about 14 doz. (Nuts make the cookies a little thicker.)

LEMON SNOWFLAKES

1 cup butter or margarine, softened
½ cup confectioner's sugar
3/4 cup cornstarch

1-1½ cup all-purpose flour
2 tsp. grated lemon rind
1 cup finely chopped nuts

Frosting:

1 cup confectioner's sugar
2 TBS. melted butter
1 TBS. lemon juice

Cream butter; combine next 4 ingredients and gradually beat into butter. Chill at least 1 hour. Shape dough in balls and drop into chopped nuts. Flatten with bottom of drinking glass dipped in flour. Put nut side up, on greased cookie sheets. Bake in preheated 350° oven about 15 minutes. Cool on rack and spread with frosting.

Recipe from *Women's Day,* Christmas, 1973.

LADYBUGS

1 cup butter or margarine, softened
3/4 cup granulated sugar
1 egg

1 tsp. vanilla
2¼ cups all-purpose flour
¼ tsp. salt

(To ⅓ dough add ½ square of melted unsweetened chocolate. Mix.)
Cream butter, add granulated sugar, mix well. Beat in egg and vanilla. Gradually stir in flour and salt. Refrigerate dough 1 hour. Preheat oven to 375° F. With floured hands, roll light-colored dough into 1-inch balls; shape each ball in a lightly floured teaspoon; slip onto greased cookie sheets about 1 inch apart.

With a knife, draw a deep line lengthwise down center of each cookie. Press 2 cherry pieces or red hots on each side of line. Shape chocolate dough into pea-size balls; flatten each on tip of a cookie to resemble head of a ladybug. Bake in 375° oven 10 minutes or until edges are lightly browned. Cool on racks.

Decorate with cinnamon red hots or chopped maraschino cherries.
Makes about 7 dozen.

Recipe adapted by Jessie Sandberg.

LEMON ANGEL HALOS

2 cups sifted all-purpose flour
1 tsp. baking soda
½ tsp. salt
2/3 cup butter or margarine
1 cup brown sugar, firmly packed
1 tsp. vanilla
1 egg

Sift together flour, soda and salt. Set aside. Cream together butter and brown sugar until light and fluffy. Add vanilla and egg. Beat well. Stir in flour mixture and blend thoroughly. Chill at least 1 hour.

Egg-White Topping:
3 egg whites (yolks to be used in filling)
3/4 cup granulated sugar
2 tsp. lemon juice

BISCUIT TORTONI

Combine ⅓ cup fine coconut macaroon crumbs, ¼ cup chopped salted almonds, 2 TBS. diced maraschino cherries (drained). Slightly soften 1 pint vanilla ice cream and fold in cherry-almond mixture. Spoon into ice cube tray or paper cups and freeze.

Dorys Gagliardi.

ENGLISH TRIFLE

3 cups broken sponge, angel or pound cake
1 pkg. strawberry Jello (large, 6-oz. size)
2 cups boiling water
1 ½ cups ice cubes
3 bananas, sliced
1 pint hulled strawberries or 1 pkg. frozen whole
1 pkg. egg custard mix*
2 cups milk
1 cup heavy cream
2 TBS. sugar
coconut, shredded
slivered almonds

1. Line the sides and bottom of an 8-cup glass serving bowl with cake.
2. Dissolve gelatin in boiling water; stir in ice cubes until melted; chill until gelatin is syrupy. Pour over cake. Chill in refrigerator for 1 hour until almost set.

Prepare custard mix with milk, following label directions. Chill for 1 hour.

4. Put sliced fruit and shredded coconut over Jello. Layer on custard.
5. Whip cream and add sugar. Cover custard and sprinkle slivered almonds over top. Serve.

*Or use custard sauce recipe given with "Lemon Snow."

RICE PUDDING

3/4 cup sugar
1 qt. milk
5 eggs
1 tsp. vanilla

½ tsp. nutmeg
½ tsp. cinnamon
2 cups cooked rice, salted

Mix first six ingredients in blender and add to rice in a large casserole. Bake for 1 hour in a 350⁰ F. oven, stirring every 15 minutes.

NOTE: If the casserole is placed in a shallow pan which contains about 1 inch of water, while it is cooking, the bottom of the pudding will not burn or become heavy.

This is a dish which is always served at the Sandberg family Smorgasbords. It is served with the main course at these affairs but you will probably want to serve it as dessert for your family.

LEMON SNOW WITH CUSTARD SAUCE

1 pkg. (3 oz.) lemon-flavor gelatin
3/4 cup boiling water
10 ice cubes
2 egg whites
Custard Sauce (recipe below)

Dissolve gelatin in boiling water. Put in blender and add ice cubes; blend at low speed until ice melts and gelatin starts to thicken. Add egg whites (saving yolks for custard sauce). Blend at high speed until mixture triples in volume and starts to hold its shape. Spoon into a 5-cup mold and chill 1 hour or until firm. Just before serving, loosen around edge with a knife; dip mold very quickly in and out of a bowl of hot water. Cover with a serving plate; turn upside down; shake gently; lift off mold. Serve with custard sauce.

Custard Sauce:
Beat egg yolks with 2 TBS. sugar and 1 tsp. cornstarch in top of double boiler; beat in 1 cup milk. Cook, stirring constantly over hot, not boiling water 10 minutes or until custard thickens slightly and coats a spoon. Remove from heat; strain into small bowl; add 1 tsp. vanilla. Chill.
NOTE: This is traditionally served at the end of the Sandberg family Christmas Smorgasbord.

MOM'S LEMON PUDDING CAKE

1 cup sugar
¼ cup flour
1/8 tsp. salt
2 TBS. melted butter
5 TBS. lemon juice

1 tsp. grated lemon rind
2 well beaten egg yolks
1 cup scalded milk
2 stiffly beaten egg whites

Combine sugar, flour, salt and butter. Add lemon juice and rind. Stir in egg yolks and milk. Mix. Fold in egg whites. Pour into greased 1½ quart dish. Bake at 325° F. until brown.
Note: This recipe may be doubled or tripled for a large family.

CHERRY CRUNCH

1 cup quick-cooking rolled oats
1 cup flour
¾ cup brown sugar
½ tsp. cinnamon
½ cup butter or margarine
1 can (22 ounce) cherry pie filling
Vanilla ice cream (optional)

Combine oats, flour, sugar and cinnamon in mixing bowl. Cut in butter with fork or pastry blender until particles are fine. Spread half the oat mixture in 9-inch square baking pan. Cover with filling and sprinkle with remaining oat mixture. Bake in preheated 375° oven 40 minutes. Serve slightly warm, topped with ice cream. Makes 9 squares.

BANANA SOUFFLE

Butter or margarine, softened
Granulated sugar
5 large eggs at room temperature, separated
1/8 tsp. salt
1 tsp. grated lemon rind
2 TBS. lemon juice
2 ripe medium bananas, sliced
2 TBS. flour
1 cup milk
1 tsp. vanilla extract
Confectioners' sugar
Sweetened whipped cream (optional)
Nutmeg (optional)

Lightly butter souffle dish (1½ quarts up to inside ridge). Sprinkle entire surface with sugar and set aside. Put egg yolks in small bowl of electric mixer and egg whites in large bowl. Add salt to whites and set aside. Combine lemon rind, lemon juice and bananas. Mash, measure 1 cup and set aside. Melt 3 TBS. butter in saucepan over medium heat and blend in flour. Gradually stir in milk and cook, stirring until smooth and thickened. Blend in ½ cup granulated sugar, vanilla and reserved bananas. Remove from heat. Beat yolks until thick and lemon-colored. Gradually add to cooked mixture, beating well. Beat whites until stiff but not dry and soft peaks form. Gradually pour cooked mixture into whites. Using rubber spatula, fold in whites lightly but evenly. Pour into souffle dish and bake in preheated 375° oven 30 to 35 minutes. Or set in pan of hot water and bake at 350° 1 hour. Sift confectioners' sugar over top and serve at once, plain or with whipped cream and a sprinkling of nutmeg. Makes 6 servings.

PARTY ICE CREAM CAKE

2 pints butter pecan and 1 pint strawberry ice cream
2 sponge 7-inch dessert layers (11 ounces)
1 cup heavy cream, whipped
2 TBS. chopped nuts

Line three 8-inch layer cake pans with foil and pack 1 pint ice cream into each. Freeze several hours or overnight. If you have only 2 pans, remove one layer when frozen, store in freezer and make another layer. Slit cake layers in half to make 4 thin layers. Put one on freezer-proof serving plate or cardboard covered with foil. Remove foil from ice cream layers; stack ice cream between layers of cake. Wrap well and return to freezer. Several hours before serving, spread with whipped cream and sprinkle with nuts. Return to freezer until serving time. If freezer is very cold, let cake stand in refrigerator about 15 minutes before serving to make slicing easier. Makes 12 to 16 servings.

LEMON-LIME SHERBET

In a small saucepan, over 1 cup milk, sprinkle 3 envelopes unflavored gelatin; heat over low fire, stirring until dissolved. Pour into freezer can. Stir in 4 cups sugar, 5 cups milk, 5 cups half-and-half, 1/3 cup grated lime peel, 1 1/2 cups lime juice, 3/4 cup lemon juice, 1 1/2 tsp. salt, 9 drops green food coloring. Freeze according to manufacturer's directions with freezer. Makes 4 quarts.

SWEET SUNFLOWER NUT TWISTS

1 pkg. active dry yeast
¼ cup warm water
¾ cup scalded milk
¼ cup sugar
½ tsp. salt
1 egg, slightly beaten
¼ cup shortening, softened
3¼ to 3¾ cups sifted all-purpose flour
¼ cup butter, melted
½ cup chopped sunflower nuts
1½ cups sifted confectioners' sugar
2 TBS. milk

Dissolve yeast in warm water. Combine milk, sugar, salt, egg and shortening. Stir into yeast mixture. Add half the flour; beat until smooth. Add enough remaining flour to form a soft dough; beat well. Turn on to lightly floured board. Knead until smooth and elastic (about 10 min.). Place in greased large bowl. Cover with damp cloth. Let rise in warm place until double in bulk, about 2 hours.

Punch down and let rise again until double in bulk, about 45 minutes. Punch down again; roll dough out on lightly floured surface into a rectangle 16 x 12 inches. Brush surface with melted butter; sprinkle with sunflower nuts. Fold ends of dough over in thirds, making an oblong three layers high. Cut dough into 24 strips about ½-inch wide. Pinch the ends of each strip together to form a circle; twist once to make a figure 8. Arrange on greased baking sheet. Cover with greased waxed paper; let rise for 30 minutes. Bake in preheated 400° oven for 10 to 12 minutes. While still warm, frost with confectioners' sugar mixed with milk.

Makes 2 dozen rolls.

RED DEVIL'S FOOD CAKE

1½ cups sifted cake flour
1 tsp. baking powder
½ tsp. salt
¼ cup shortening
1 cup sugar
2 eggs, well beaten
½ cup buttermilk
½ cup boiling water
2 squares bitter chocolate, melted
1 tsp. soda
1 tsp. vanilla

Mix by hand; don't overbeat. Sift flour before measuring. Add baking powder and salt; sift together *three* times. Set aside. Cream shortening and sugar together by hand.

Use a rotary hand beater for the eggs and combine with sugar and shortening. Blend in flour and buttermilk alternately, in small amounts, mixing with your spoon after each addition.

Melt chocolate in a double boiler. Use a pan large enough to contain about 2 cups, because it is going to foam up.

Pour the boiling water into the melted chocolate; stir until smooth. Add soda; continue stirring until thick. Combine with batter. Add vanilla and stir.

Bake in a 9 x 9 in. well-greased, square pan for 25-30 min. at 350°.

It is done when it pulls away slightly at the edge, or when light finger pressure at center fails to make a lasting dent, or when a toothpick comes out clean.

FUDGE FROSTING

1 ½ cups granulated sugar
2/3 cup milk
2 squares bitter chocolate
1 TBS. honey or light corn syrup
Dash salt
1 tsp. vanilla
2 TBS. butter

Combine first five ingredients in large saucepan and place over medium heat. Stir until sugar is dissolved. Continue cooking until a small amount forms a soft ball in a cup of cold water, or reaches a temperature of 232 degrees on a candy thermometer. Remove from heat; add butter and vanilla.

Let cool until pan feels lukewarm or frosting reaches 110 degrees. You may set the pan in cold water to hasten the cooling. Beat frosting until it is creamy and just begins to hold its shape. Spread quickly on top and sides of 9-inch square cake.

For a party, double the recipe and bake in three layers. Spread raspberry jam between the layers and frost liberally with a double recipe of Fudge Frosting.

PECAN TEA LOAF

½ cup milk (scalded)
½ cup butter
½ tsp. salt
¼ cup sugar
2 yeast cakes or 2 pkgs. dry yeast
3¼ to 3½ cups all-purpose flour
2 whole eggs (well-beaten)
1 cup pecan pieces, chopped

To the scalded milk, add butter, salt, and sugar. When cooled to lukewarm, stir in yeast, which has been dissolved in the lukewarm water. Add half of the flour.

Beat to a smooth batter while stirring in the eggs alternately with the remainder of the flour, holding out ½ cup flour.

Let rise in warm place to double in bulk. Turn dough out on a lightly-floured board and knead until smooth and satiny. During kneading, add flour held out, so you can handle dough better. It will be very soft.

Work in the cup of pecan pieces until well-dispersed. Return to bowl and let rise again until double. Shape into two loaves and place in bread pans.

Let rise again until double in size. Bake in 350° oven until done (up to

45 minutes). May be frosted with a simple white icing with whole pecans arranged on top.

BLUEBERRY DESSERT

Line 9 x 9-inch, buttered pan with vanilla wafer crumbs. In a double boiler mix 1 cup powdered sugar, 1 stick oleo, 2 slightly beaten eggs. Stir often and cook until thickened (for about 30 minutes). When cool, pour into pan over crumbs. Sprinkle with finely chopped nuts. Spread 1 can blueberry pie filling over nuts, and 1 pint whipped cream or frozen whipped topping over filling. Sprinkle with vanilla wafer crumbs. Let set several hours or over night in refrigerator.

LOW CALORIE LIME REFRESHER

1 small pkg. lime-flavored gelatin
¾ cup hot water
½ cup sugar
3 TBS. lemon juice
1½ tsp. grated lemon peel
1½ cup buttermilk
1 stiff-beaten egg white

Dissolve gelatin in hot water. Add sugar; stir to dissolve. Stir in juice, peel, and buttermilk. Pour into refrigerator tray; freeze firm. Break into chunks; beat with electric beater till smooth. Fold in egg white. Freeze firm. Serves 6.

CREAMY BANANA DESSERT

1 cup butter or magarine (reserve half)
1½ cups graham cracker or vanilla wafer crumbs
2 eggs
2 cups powdered sugar
1 tsp. vanilla extract
4 bananas, sliced
1 can (20-ounce) crushed pineapple, drained
1½ cup heavy cream, whipped and sweetened (or substitute frozen whipped topping)
½ cup chopped pecans or walnuts

Melt ½ cup butter and mix with graham cracker crumbs. Pat into 13 x 9-inch pan.

Combine sugar, eggs, ½ cup softened butter, and vanilla; mix until smooth and creamy. Spread over graham cracker crust. Add a layer of banana slices and pineapple; spread whipped cream evenly over fruit. Sprinkle with nuts and refrigerate until set. Serves 12-15.

LOUISIANA PRALINE CRUNCH
(To be served over ice cream)

½ cup butter (1 stick)   *½ cup pecans, broken*
1 cup brown sugar, packed   *2½ cups cornflakes*

Place butter and sugar in saucepan and bring to a boil; boil just two minutes. Add nuts and cornflakes and toss with a fork to coat with the syrup. Cool and serve over vanilla ice cream. (This will keep for a long time if stored in a plastic bag.)

A BIBLE CAKE

4½ cups—I Sam. 28:24 (all purpose flour)
2 tsp.—Lev. 23:17 (baking powder)
pinch of Luke 14:34 (salt)
3 tsps.—Exod. 37:29 (1 tsp. each cinnamon, allspice, nutmeg, ground)
1 cup (2 sticks)—Judges 5:25 (butter, or substitute margarine)
2 cups—Jer. 6:20 (sugar)
6 large—Luke 11:12 (eggs; no scorpions, please!)
2 TBS—Prov. 25:27 (honey)
½ cup—I Cor. 3:2 (milk)
2 cups Nahum 3:12—cut up (figs, or substitute prunes)
2 cups coarseley chopped, unblanched—Numbers 17:8 (almonds)

Heat oven to 350⁰ F. Grease a 13 x 9-in. baking pan with unsalted shortening. Sift flour with salt, baking powder, cinnamon, allspice and nutmeg. In the large bowl of an electric mixer beat butter at medium speed until soft and creamy. Add sugar, a little at a time, mixing well between times. Add eggs one at a time, beating well. Reduce speed of mixer, add honey and then mix in sifted dry ingredients a little at a time alternating with milk. Remove from mixer and stir in figs and almonds with spoon. Pour batter into prepared pan. Bake 50 to 60 minutes, until cake springs back when lightly touched. Turn out cake onto a wire rack and cool completely. Makes 36 pieces. Needs no frosting.

CHOCOLATE VELVET

8 oz. semi-sweet chocolate bits   *1/8 tsp. salt*
1½ cups milk   *½ cup light cream*
1½ envelopes unflavored gelatin   *½ tsp. vanilla*
½ cup cold water   *¼ tsp. almond extract*
½ cup sugar   *1 cup heavy cream, whipped*

Put chocolate pieces and milk in double boiler and scald until chocolate melts. Soften gelatin in cold water. Beat chocolate and milk with rotary beater. Add softened gelatin, ½ cup sugar and salt. Stir until dissolved. Add light cream, ½ tsp. vanilla, ½ tsp. almond extract and 1 cup heavy cream, whipped. Mix until smooth. Chill in five cup ring mold until firm. Remove from mold and frost with sour cream frosting.

SOUR CREAM FROSTING

8 oz. semi-sweet chocolate bits   *8 oz. sour cream*
2 tsp. instant coffee

Melt chocolate bits in double boiler. Stir in sour cream and instant coffee. Frost chocolate velvet dessert after it has been unmolded. Serves 8. (Mold can be prepared a day or two in advance of using; keep under refrigeration.)

SNOW BALL CAKE
(A Chattanooga Favorite)

2 envelopes plain gelatin   *1 medium size angel food cake*
2 cups crushed pineapple   *1 can angel flake coconut*
1 cup sugar   *3 small boxes Dream Whip*
½ tsp. salt   *juice of 1 large lemon*

Dissolve the gelatin in 4 tablespoons ice water. Add 1 cup boiling water. Stir and set aside to cool. Combine pineapple, sugar, salt and lemon to the cooled gelatin. Let partially congeal and fold in two boxes of Dream Whip (which have been whipped according to the directions on the box.) Break cake in bite size pieces—removing any brown crust. Line a bowl or pyrex dish (14 x 9 in.) with wax paper. Layer. Begin and end with the mixture. Let stand overnight in the refrigerator. Turn out on cake plate. Remove wax paper. Frost with the other box of Dream Whip. Sprinkle with coconut. Store in the refrigerator.

SCANDINAVIAN APPLE BARS

2½ cups sifted flour
½ tsp. salt
1 cup butter or margarine
1 egg yolk
          . . .
1 cup cornflakes
8 to 10 tart apples, peeled and sliced (about 8 cups)
¾ cup sugar
1 tsp. ground cinnamon
1 egg white

Combine flour and salt; cut in butter. Beat egg yolk in measuring cup; add enough milk to make 2/3 cup liquid. Mix well; stir into flour mixture.

On floured surface, roll half the dough to 17 x 12 inch rectangle; fit into and up sides of 14 x 9 (or 15½ x 10½ inch) baking pan. Sprinkle with cornflakes; top with apple. Combine sugar and cinnamon; sprinkle on top. Roll remaining dough to fit pan; place over apples. Seal edges; cut slits in top. Beat egg white until frothy; brush on crust. Bake in 375⁰ oven 50 minutes. Combine 1 cup sifted powdered sugar and 3 to 4 teaspoons milk, drizzle on warm bars. Makes 3 dozen.

HOT FUDGE PUDDING

1 cup sifted flour
2 tsp. baking powder
pinch of salt
¾ cup sugar
2 TBS. cocoa
½ cup milk
2 TBS. butter or margarine, melted
1 cup chopped nuts
1 cup brown sugar (packed)
1¾ cups hot water

Heat oven to 350⁰. Sift flour, baking powder, salt, sugar and 2 TBS. cocoa into bowl. Stir in milk and butter. Blend in nuts. Spread in square pan (approx. 9 x 9 inch). Sprinkle with brown sugar, cocoa mixture. Pour hot water over entire batter. Bake 45 min. During baking, cake mixture rises to top and chocolate sauce settles in bottom of pan. Serve warm, spooned into saucedishes, with whipped cream. 9 servings.

CINNAMON APPLES

8 apples cored and peeled
1½ cups sugar
2 TBS. butter
½ cup red cinnamon drops

Make syrup of sugar, water, butter and cinnamon drops; cook 5 or 10 minutes until drops dissolve. Add apples; cook slowly until tender. Turn and baste with the syrup until they are a pretty red color and clear in appearance. Remove from heat; pour syrup around apples. Delicious served cold with cream.

Books for the Youngsters

Those Kids in Proverbsville

By Elizabeth Rice Handford. Scriptural, moralizing stories for children. As the title suggests, these interesting, true-to-life episodes are based on inspired axioms from the book of Proverbs. Each of the 20 short stories is illustrated with drawings by a noted artist. Paper-bound, glossy cover, 93 pages.

A Reward for Jerry

By Grace Rice MacMullen. Christian fiction story for children, containing elements of excitement, mystery, adventure, and humor together with examples of soul winning and revival cleverly and interestingly woven into the warp and woof of the story. Illustrated, 96 pages,

---

The Exiled Prince

By Elizabeth Rice Handford. This volume, ran serially in THE SWORD OF THE LORD, has not only the age-old interesting and challenging "story of Daniel from captive lad to prime minister of the world empires" to grip the attention of children, but a wealth of material for any serious-minded Bible student. 14 chapters 106 pp.

The Exiled Prince

The Story of Daniel From Captive Lad to Prime Minister of World Empires

By Elizabeth Rice Handford

A Bible Story for Children of All Ages!

Dr. Robert L. Sumner, noted evangelist, says:

Here is a historical/scriptural novel dealing with the life of the Prophet Daniel from his youthful captivity to his exalted position as the number two man in the mightiest empires the world has ever known. Mrs. Handford has done a superb job of researching and the story flows so smoothly and interestingly that, although written for children and young people, adults will find it fascinating.

Young people must have their heroes. If you have any kids around your house—especially in the junior/junior high age bracket—we suggest you get this book for them to read. It will whet their interest in Scripture, strengthen their character, and, who knows, maybe they'll *dare to be Daniels*, too.

Two Other Success Books

Me? Obey Him?

By Elizabeth Rice Handford

Here is a book about women, for women, by a woman! It is tremendous! We doubt not that this book, placed in the right hands, could revolutionize a homelife that had been a hovel of misery and transform it into a haven of happiness. It could turn a defeated, frustrated, miserable wife into a happy, contented, excited helpmate. It could save many a home already on the verge of divorce. An investment in this book will pay big dividends. An ideal gift suggestion.

The Right Romance in Marriage
By Cathy Rice

This book has proven to be an extremely valuable one. Literally hundreds of letters have told of ruined marriages being saved from divorce courts, of dull marriages that have regained the fervor and excitement of honeymoon days and unhappy marriages that have found the answer to their problems. Many pastors now make it a practice to give a copy of this book to each couple they marry in order that the newlyweds may begin their life together.